HOPE'S TABLE

HOPE'S TABLE

EVERYDAY RECIPES *from a* MENNONITE KITCHEN

HOPE HELMUTH

H̶ERALD
PRESS

Harrisonburg, Virginia

Herald Press
PO Box 866, Harrisonburg, Virginia 22803
www.HeraldPress.com

Library of Congress Cataloging-in-Publication Data
Names: Helmuth, Hope, author.
Title: Hope's table : everyday recipes from a Mennonite kitchen / Hope Helmuth.
Description: Harrisonburg, Virginia : Herald Press, 2019. | Includes index.
Identifiers: LCCN 2018052384| ISBN 9781513803234 (hardcover : alk. paper)
Subjects: LCSH: Mennonite cooking. | LCGFT: Cookbooks.
Classification: LCC TX715 .H458 2019 | DDC 641.5/66--dc23 LC record available at
https://lccn.loc.gov/2018052384

HOPE'S TABLE
© 2019 by Herald Press, Harrisonburg, Virginia 22803. 800-245-7894. All rights reserved.
Library of Congress Control Number: 2018052384
International Standard Book Number: 978-1-5138-0323-4 (hardcover); 978-1-5138-0324-1 (ebook)
Printed in China
Photography: Sera Petras (cover, back cover author photo, pp. 1, 2, 6, 7, 8, 312, 318, 319); Lana
Whetzel (pp. 4, 5, 20, 311); all other photos by Hope Helmuth. *Cover:* Herb Roasted Chicken
Thighs and Potatoes (see p. 209). *Back cover:* Ranch Dressing (see p. 92), Slow-Baked Macaroni
(see p. 115), Cinnamon Rolls with Caramel Icing (see p. 19).

27 26 25 24 23   18 17 16 15 14

For my girls:
may you find joy
in everyday cooking

CONTENTS

INTRODUCTION

Hello! I am so glad you opened this book. I'm a stay-at-home housewife and mom. I have a passion for cooking, creating recipes, and entertaining guests. Cooking truly is one of my love languages. I just love to cook for my family and anyone who enters our home.

My husband, Joshua, and I and our children live in the Shenandoah Valley of Virginia, where we are surrounded by our families and community, which are rich in our Mennonite faith. We live in a Swiss chalet that Joshua's grandfather built. It's nestled among pine trees, and there is a river running through the front of our property.

I grew up on a farm, helping my mom and dad work in our garden. I think it's important for this generation to learn where their food comes from and how to cook wholesome meals. To be a good cook, you don't have to have a spacious kitchen with the most expensive tools. You need basic ingredients, a fridge, a stove, an oven, and a willing mind to learn.

As my mom says, "Half the taste of food is the presentation." I believe God gave us all the colorful fruits and vegetables for us to enjoy and to create beautiful things with. My mom taught me how to create meals with color and that a little sprig of parsley added as a garnish can brighten up anything.

These recipes are a collection of what I grew up eating and new recipes I have created. These recipes are from scratch and can be made mostly with what you have in your pantry or refrigerator. I'm a last-minute, practical cook, but I also like things to taste good and look appetizing. I don't claim to be a cooking expert, but I want to share the recipes with you that my family enjoys.

I have a passion for my Mennonite heritage and want to help preserve it. I do think that my heritage of cooking is slowly being lost. The busyness that this era brings makes it hard to keep some traditions—like eating meals together as a family—alive. I encourage you to gather your family and friends around your table. Community is so important for the health of your family. This era brings so much pressure to be doing all the things everyone else is doing. But a community environment is much more important than all the scheduled activities children do nowadays. We need to teach our children how to rest and enjoy the small but important things in life—like gathering around a table and sharing a home-cooked meal with family and friends.

Last but not least, I am a follower of Christ. Without Jesus, I am nothing. May all the glory be given to God. More than anything, I desire to do God's will while I am on this earth. "Thou art worthy, O Lord, to receive glory and honour and power: for thou hast created all things, and for thy pleasure they are and were created" (Revelation 4:11 KJV).

With love,

Hope

BREAKFAST

I'm not a morning person. That's hard to admit, but I've decided to embrace that fact. Still, I try to be disciplined and to be cheerful in the mornings. So you'll understand why I don't fix elaborate breakfasts. We usually have fried *pon haus* (you can read more about that on p. 164) or sausage and eggs. Some weekends I mix up waffle batter and use that same batter the whole weekend. It keeps just fine in the refrigerator. On special weekends, I make sausage gravy and fried apples.

But the most important thing? That hot coffee mug I hug while making breakfast.

Simple Granola

Waffles

Sausage Gravy

Fried Apples

Cinnamon Rolls with Caramel Icing

Fiesta Lime Omelet

Soft Baked Eggs

Basic Quiche

Sausage Potato Quiche

Potato Nest Skillet

SIMPLE GRANOLA

Serves 6

This granola is great with milk or in a parfait with yogurt and fresh fruit. We give this grano-la to our Airbnb guests. They love it, and some even eat the whole jarful before they leave. I choose not to add dried fruit to my granola, because my jaws get tired from chewing it! But you could add some dried fruits after the granola is baked and cooled.

6 cups rolled oats

1 cup chopped pecans

1½ cup shredded coconut

¼ cup butter, melted

½ cup canola oil

½ cup maple syrup

½ packed cup brown sugar

1½ teaspoon salt

1 teaspoon ground cinnamon

½ teaspoon vanilla extract

In a large mixing bowl, combine rolled oats, pecans, and coconut. In a separate bowl, mix together remaining ingredients. Pour over rolled oat mixture and mix well.

Pour granola onto a baking sheet lined with parchment paper. Spread out evenly. Bake at 300°F for 45 minutes to 1 hour, or just until golden brown (ovens seem to make a difference on this recipe). Do not stir. Remove from oven and let cool completely. You will need to break the granola into smaller clumps for storage. Place in airtight container to keep fresh.

WAFFLES

Serves 6

These waffles are quick and delicious. You can mix them up the night before and refrigerate the batter overnight. This batter also works great for pancakes. If making several waffles at a time, heat your oven to 200°F and place the waffles in a single layer on a baking sheet in the oven while baking the remaining waffles. This helps them to stay warm and crisp.

---

1 cup unbleached white flour

1 cup white whole wheat flour

1 tablespoon sugar

1 tablespoon baking powder

1 teaspoon salt

1¾ cup milk

2 eggs, beaten

¼ cup sour cream

¼ cup butter, melted

In a medium bowl, mix together the white flour, whole wheat flour, sugar, baking powder, and salt. Make well in center of the flour mixture; set aside. In another bowl, beat together milk, eggs, and sour cream. Pour milk mixture into flour mixture and mix just until combined (it's okay if there are some clumps). Fold in melted butter. Bake in hot waffle iron for waffles or on a griddle for pancakes.

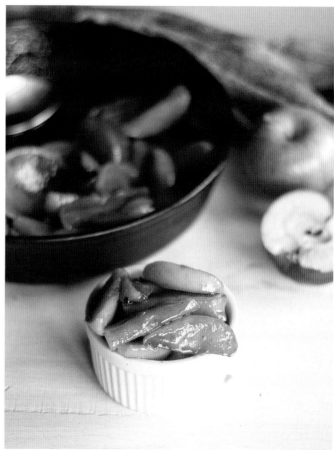

SAUSAGE GRAVY

Serves 4

If you want your family to jump out of bed in the morning, make sausage gravy. I serve it over pancakes, waffles, or biscuits.

---

1 pound ground pork sausage

½ cup unbleached white flour

4 cups milk

salt and pepper

In a large skillet, brown sausage. Stir in flour and keep stirring until most of it is dissolved. Pour in milk while stirring constantly. Simmer on low heat until gravy is thickened. Season to taste with salt and pepper. If the gravy is too thick, add more milk.

FRIED APPLES

Serves 4–6

These are a tasty side to a savory breakfast dish. They are also good on waffles with sausage gravy. I like to use Gala apples.

¼ cup butter

6 apples, sliced

2 teaspoons lemon juice

⅓ packed cup brown sugar

¼ teaspoon salt

1 teaspoon ground cinnamon

dash ground nutmeg

In a cast iron skillet, melt butter and then add apples. Sprinkle with lemon juice, brown sugar, and salt. Cover and cook on medium-low for 10 minutes, or until apples are just tender. Remove lid and sprinkle with cinnamon and nutmeg. If a lot of liquid remains, turn heat to high and cook liquid down until it reduces.

CINNAMON ROLLS
with Caramel Icing
Makes 3–4 dozen rolls

Cinnamon rolls, smothered with caramel icing, are a favorite of mine. Freeze them the same day you bake them—even if you are planning to serve them the next day. When frozen, they retain their freshness. A day-old cinnamon roll just isn't the same! Also, be sure not to over-bake the rolls.

Rolls

2 cups warm water

¼ cup active dry yeast

1 tablespoon granulated sugar

¾ cup butter, softened

1 cup granulated sugar

4 eggs

2 teaspoons vanilla extract

1 tablespoon salt

8½ cups unbleached white flour

Filling

½ cup butter, melted

⅔ cup brown sugar

2 tablespoons ground cinnamon

In a medium bowl, mix together water, yeast, and 1 tablespoon granulated sugar. Set aside.

Using a stand mixer fitted with the wire whip, cream butter and 1 cup granulated sugar until fluffy. Add eggs, one at a time, then add vanilla and salt. Add yeast mixture. Switch to the dough hook attachment on your mixer; add flour. Knead until smooth. The dough will be sticky. Place dough in a large, greased bowl and cover. Let rise until doubled.

Divide dough in half. On floured surface, roll out dough into a 12 x 24-inch rectangle. Spread half the melted butter on first rectangle and sprinkle with half the brown sugar and cinnamon. Roll up lengthwise and pinch seams well. With a string, cut into circles about 1 inch thick. Place rolls in a greased 9 x 13-inch baking dish (or baking pan of your choice) and cover with a light cloth. Repeat this step for the remaining dough. Let rise until doubled, around 40 minutes. Bake at 350°F for 15–20 minutes, or until internal temperature reaches 190°F. The baking time may differ with your choice of pan or how thick the rolls are cut.

Caramel icing

¾ cup butter

1½ cup brown sugar

⅔ cup milk

2 cups powdered sugar

1 teaspoon vanilla extract

pinch salt

In a saucepan, melt butter, add brown sugar, and boil for 1 minute. Add milk and return to a boil. Remove from heat. Cool 5 minutes. Add powdered sugar, vanilla, and salt. Whisk until smooth. Spread on warm rolls.

Teaching children about food

Growing up, we ate what was set on the table in front of us. Mom didn't fix "kid friendly" meals or cater to our tastes. We ate normal, wholesome meals—usually with beef from the farm, milk from our dairy, eggs from my uncle's farm, and vegetables from our garden.

We were those kids at school with the uncool lunches. I credit my mom for not buying into what was easy or trendy but just sending along leftovers from supper the night before or a simple sandwich. We also didn't have unhealthy snacks at home or lots of baked goods to eat. I remember eating Mom's canned pickles and cheese or leftovers for snacks after school.

We always had a large garden, and my siblings and I helped weed, plant, pick, and preserve produce. We were always the most helpful on days that we were told we could go swimming afterward. I remember picking rocks on the first day of summer vacation from school. As Dad would say, "It builds character." My grandmas would often come over to help us snap green beans, shell limas, work sweet corn, or can peaches.

Now that I have children of my own, I feel a great responsibility to pass on my heritage of food to them. My husband and I have a garden,

and our daughter Caroline loves to help pick produce. We are still working on developing her love for weeding.

It seems like academic skills are being pushed on children at a younger age these days. I say let children be children and learn life skills before first grade. Young children can learn how to be responsible and feed their pet, how to clean up after themselves, how to make simple foods, and how to respect authority figures—whether it's a parent, a grandparent, or a neighbor.

One way I have let Caroline help in the kitchen is premeasuring ingredients for a simple recipe like Protein Balls (p. 283) and letting her pour all the ingredients together and mix them. She has started to help make her dad's egg sandwiches for his work breakfast, and she seems to receive great joy from helping make his food. Anytime the mixer is turned on in our house, you can bet a little girl will come and ask to sit on the counter and help.

It's not always easy letting Caroline help, or teaching her to be responsible. But she is a child, and she needs to be taught by us. We are not perfect parents by any means, but these are some things we strive for.

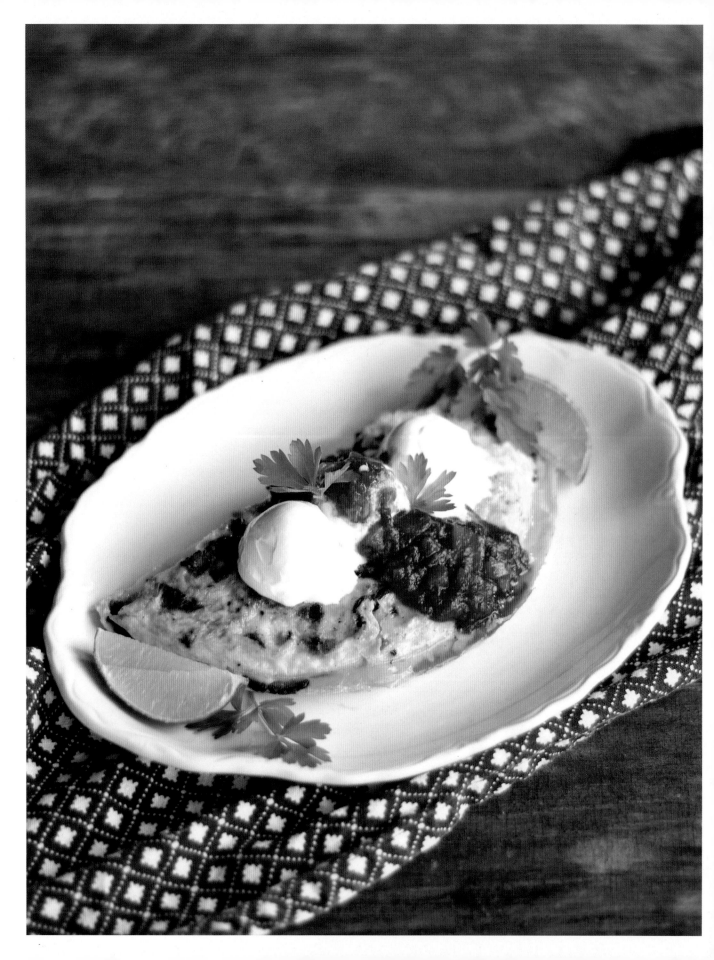

FIESTA LIME OMELET

Serves 2

A flavor-filled omelet that Joshua loves. The combination of sour cream and salsa on eggs is simply wonderful.

3 slices bacon

¼ onion, sliced

½ jalapeño pepper, sliced

5 eggs

2 tablespoons milk

salt and pepper

1 lime

½ cup shredded cheddar cheese

¼ cup sour cream

¼ cup salsa

parsley or cilantro, for garnish

Use kitchen scissors to snip bacon into small pieces and drop in a nonstick skillet. Fry bacon on medium heat until almost done. Add onion and jalapeño pepper. Sauté until tender.

In a small bowl, beat eggs and milk, and sprinkle in a dash salt and pepper. Add egg mixture to skillet. Cover and cook on low until omelet is set. Squeeze juice of half a lime onto omelet. Then cover half the omelet with cheese. Using a spatula, fold in half.

Slide omelet onto a serving plate. Add a dollop of sour cream and salsa. Garnish with fresh parsley or cilantro, and slice the remaining lime half into wedges and serve.

SOFT BAKED EGGS

Serves 4–6

An easy way to fix a dozen eggs for breakfast. It's simple and delicious.

---

1 pound ground pork sausage

1 cup shredded Monterey Jack cheese

12 eggs

½ cup heavy cream

salt and pepper

fresh basil, chopped

In a skillet, brown sausage. Spread browned sausage on the bottom of a 9 x 13-inch baking dish. Sprinkle with cheese and crack eggs on top. Pour heavy cream evenly over the eggs and sprinkle with a dash salt and pepper. Bake at 350°F for 15–20 minutes. Remove from oven before the eggs are set, because they will continue to cook. Sprinkle with basil, and serve.

BASIC QUICHE

Serves 4–6

Quiche is delicious served hot or cold. I like how versatile it is. You can use different meats, vegetables, and cheeses. Just be sure to cook raw vegetables before adding them to the pie shell so the juices release before baking. You don't want a soggy quiche!

½ onion, sliced

2 cups spinach

1 (9-inch) unbaked pie shell

8 slices bacon, fried and chopped, or 1 cup ground pork sausage, browned

1½ cup shredded cheddar or Gouda cheese

3 eggs

2 cups half-and-half

½ teaspoon salt

freshly ground pepper, as desired

In a skillet, heat a little oil and sauté onions until translucent. Add spinach. Stir until wilted, then drain.

In an unbaked pie shell, layer spinach, onions, meat of choice, and cheese. In a small bowl, beat together eggs, half-and-half, salt, and pepper. Pour over top. Bake at 375°F for 30 minutes. Let stand 10 minutes before slicing.

SAUSAGE POTATO QUICHE

Serves 4–6

I grew up eating this quiche for supper, not only breakfast. It's hearty and delicious.

Crust

3 cups uncooked shredded potatoes

½ cup chopped onion

3 tablespoons oil

Filling

2 eggs, beaten

1 cup milk or cream

½ teaspoon salt

½ teaspoon pepper

2 cups ground pork sausage, browned

1½ cup shredded cheddar cheese

1 fresh tomato, chopped

1 tablespoon fresh parsley, or 1 teaspoon dried parsley flakes

In a small bowl, mix together shredded potatoes, onions, and oil. Press into a 9-inch deep-dish pie pan. Bake at 400°F until browned (about 12 minutes).

In a small bowl, beat eggs, milk or cream, salt, and pepper.

Remove potato crust from the oven and sprinkle with sausage, cheese, and tomato. Pour egg mixture over top and sprinkle with parsley. Bake at 350°F for 40 minutes; let rest 5 minutes before serving, so the egg mixture can set.

POTATO NEST SKILLET

Serves 4

I love fried potatoes for breakfast. You can also use leftover baked, roasted potatoes or pre-shredded hash browns. Sauté onions then add pre-cooked potatoes. Season with salt and pepper and skip ahead to making nests for the eggs.

3 medium potatoes

2 tablespoons oil

¼ cup chopped onions

salt and pepper

6 eggs

¼ cup half-and-half

½ cup shredded Monterey Jack cheese

Slice potatoes into thin matchsticks. In a skillet, heat oil over medium heat. Add potatoes and onions. Stir often to prevent potatoes from sticking (you can add a little water to loosen up the pan bottom, if needed).

Once the potatoes are tender, sprinkle with salt and pepper and stir well. Then make six "nests" for the eggs. Add an egg to each nest and sprinkle each egg yolk with a little additional salt. Top with half-and-half. Reduce heat to low, cover, and cook until eggs are almost set. Top with cheese. Turn off heat and cover again until the cheese is melted.

BREADS

There is nothing like walking into a kitchen filled with the smell of freshly baked bread. I didn't bake bread until we got married, but I have learned over the years, by trial and error. Now I can bake bread that looks nice enough to give away.

I used to struggle with shaping my bread loaves and finally learned to roll out the dough as long as my bread pan, brush the top with water, and roll it up like a jelly roll. These steps help to ensure a nice inside texture free from air pockets.

When I bake bread, it seems half a loaf is eaten before that fresh-baked bread smell has even left my kitchen. But then I remember that's why I baked it in the first place: to nourish the ones I love.

Blueberry and White Chocolate Scones

Aunt Shirley's Corn Bread

Belizean Fry Jacks

French Bread

Easy Sourdough Bread

Mom's Rolls

Pretzel Buns

Cheesy Breadsticks

BLUEBERRY AND WHITE CHOCOLATE SCONES

Makes 8 scones

This recipe is from a good friend, Amy, who makes the best scones. You can use other kinds of frozen fruit. Great for an afternoon coffee break on a rainy day.

2 cups unbleached white flour

⅓ cup sugar, plus additional for sprinkling

1 tablespoon baking powder

½ teaspoon salt

6 tablespoons cold butter, grated

½ cup frozen blueberries

¼ cup white chocolate chips

½–¾ cup heavy cream

In a medium bowl, mix together flour, ⅓ cup sugar, baking powder, and salt. Cut in grated butter and mix until coarse. Add fruit and white chocolate chips. Using your hands to mix, add cream ¼ cup at a time until mixture comes together and forms a ball. Form dough into a 7-inch circle and wrap in plastic wrap. Refrigerate until stiff. Cut into 8 wedges. Place scones on baking sheet lined with parchment paper. Brush tops with heavy cream and sprinkle with additional sugar. Bake at 400°F for 15–18 minutes, or until starting to brown.

AUNT SHIRLEY'S CORN BREAD

Serves 8

This recipe comes from my aunt Shirley. Anyone who tries it falls in love with the taste and texture.

1 cup unbleached white flour

¾ cup cornmeal

3 tablespoons sugar

1 teaspoon baking soda

1 teaspoon baking powder

½ teaspoon salt

2 eggs

1 cup sour cream

¾ cup buttermilk

2 tablespoons butter, melted

In a medium-sized bowl, mix together ingredients in order listed. Pour into a greased 9-inch cast iron skillet, 9-inch baking dish, or muffin cups. Bake at 350°F for 20–25 minutes (until wooden pick inserted in the center comes out clean), or 14 minutes for muffin cups. Serve warm with butter and honey.

BELIZEAN FRY JACKS

Serves 6

In my teenage years, a student from Belize named Lynette lived with my family. Years later, we consider her part of our family and I call her my sister. Lynette makes the best fry jacks. This dough also makes wonderful tortillas.

2 cups unbleached white flour

1½ teaspoon baking powder

½ heaping teaspoon salt

1 tablespoon cold butter

½–¾ cup cold water

canola oil, for frying

In a small bowl, mix together flour, baking powder, and salt with your hands. Cut in butter until largest pieces are the size of a pea. Add ½ cup cold water and keep stirring with your hands, adding just enough additional water for the dough to come together. Knead until smooth. The dough should be soft and elastic but not sticky. Form into 8 balls. Place in a container and cover. Refrigerate for 10–15 minutes or overnight.

In a medium-sized saucepan, heat 2 inches canola oil.

Using minimal flour, roll each ball into a thin circle. Cut into thirds. Test heat of oil with one piece of fry jack; if the dough doesn't bubble up right away or if it starts sinking, the oil is not hot enough. Once the oil is hot, fry on both sides until golden brown. Place in a bowl lined with paper towels. Serve immediately. Fry jacks are good with rice and chicken, or you can eat them with jam.

For tortillas: After kneading, form dough into 6 balls. Place in fridge for 10–15 minutes or overnight. Using minimal flour, roll into a thin circle. In hot skillet with a bit of oil, fry on each side until starting to bubble and brown. Remove from heat and cover with a heavy cloth while you make the rest.

FRENCH BREAD

Makes 2 long loaves

This is the first bread I tried to make when I was a young cook, and it's still a favorite of mine to make. This French bread is soft and fluffy, and it's hard to stop eating it when it's fresh out of the oven. I use this same dough for rolls and sandwich bread. It makes about 27 (2-ounce) rolls or 2 nice loaves of sandwich bread.

2½ cups warm water

2 tablespoons active dry yeast

2 tablespoons sugar

3 tablespoons butter, melted

2 teaspoons salt

1 tablespoon sunflower lecithin*
  (optional)

6–7 cups unbleached white flour

1 egg, beaten

1 tablespoon water

Using a stand mixer fitted with a dough hook, mix together warm water, yeast, and sugar. Let rest until yeast foams. Add butter, salt, and lecithin, if desired. With mixer on low, start adding flour 2 cups at a time. Mix until the dough pulls away from the sides of the mixing bowl and is smooth, around 5 minutes. Place dough in a large greased bowl; cover tightly with plastic wrap. Let rise until doubled in size, punch down, and let rise again until doubled in size.

Divide dough in half. Roll each half into a 10 x 14-inch rectangle. Brush outside edges with water. Roll up and pinch seam edges tight. Place dough seam side down on a greased baking sheet. Cover with a light cloth. Let rise until doubled in size.

In a small bowl, beat egg and water and then brush over loaf tops. Using a sharp knife, make six ¼-inch-deep diagonal slashes across the top of each loaf. Bake at 350°F for 25 minutes, or until the center registers 195°F. Remove from oven and brush tops with additional butter. Cool on wire racks. Slice in thick slices and serve.

*Lecithin increases tenderness and improves the shelf life of breads.

EASY SOURDOUGH BREAD

Makes 2 sandwich bread loaves

This bread is wonderful and easy to make. Sourdough bread has a delightful chewy texture and a lovely tang at the end. The dough can be used for many other things. This recipe is tweaked from Glenda Groff's cookbook Around the Family Table. *Sourdough starter can be purchased online—better yet, ask for a starter from a friend who bakes with sourdough.*

2 cups unfed sourdough starter

1 cup water

½ cup milk

2 tablespoons butter, melted

2 tablespoons honey

5–5½ cups unbleached white flour

1 tablespoon sunflower lecithin*
(optional)

2½ teaspoons salt

Using a stand mixer fitted with the dough hook, mix together the sourdough starter, water, milk, butter, honey, flour and sunflower lecithin. Knead for 3 minutes. Cover the mixing bowl with a cloth and let dough rest for 30 minutes.

Uncover, add salt, and knead for 5 minutes more. Place dough in a large greased bowl. Cover tightly with lid or plastic wrap and let rise 4 hours.

FOR BREAD:
Divide dough in half and shape into 2 loaves. Place in two greased bread pans. Place each loaf in a large plastic bag, securing the ends. Let rise until bread has risen about 1½ inch above the pan rim. Remove plastic bags. Score loaves and bake at 375°F for 25–30 minutes, or until the center registers 195°F. Cool on baking racks and freeze one loaf for later in the week.

FOR A CHEWIER ARTISAN BREAD TEXTURE:
After the first 4-hour rise and you have shaped your loaves, place each loaf in a large plastic bag and secure the ends. Refrigerate for 12 hours. Remove from refrigerator and let rise until dough has risen about 1½ inch above the pan rim.

Remove plastic bags. Score loaves and bake at 375°F for 25–30 minutes, or until the center registers 195°F.

FOR PIZZA:
This dough also makes wonderful pizza crust. You can make pizza crust after the first 4-hour rise, or for a chewier texture, you can place dough in a bowl covered with a lid and ferment for several days more in the refrigerator. After the desired rise time, line two baking sheets with parchment paper and drizzle with olive oil. Halve the dough and press each half onto a baking sheet, up to 1–2 inches away from the sides of the sheets. Top with pizza sauce, shredded mozzarella cheese, and toppings. Bake at 475°F for 12–15 minutes.

*Lecithin increases tenderness in bread and improves the shelf life of breads.

MOM'S ROLLS

Makes about 3 dozen rolls

These rolls were present all through my childhood. When company came over, we served the rolls with butter and jam. When we had youth parties at our house, the rolls were filled with shaved ham and cheese.

4 cups unbleached white flour

2 cups whole wheat flour

¾ cup sugar

2 teaspoons salt

1 cup warm water

1 tablespoon active dry yeast

1 cup mashed potatoes

½ cup lard (or butter)

3 eggs, beaten

In a large mixing bowl, combine white flour, whole wheat flour, sugar, and salt. Make a well in the middle and add warm water and yeast. Let stand until yeast begins to foam.

In another mixing bowl, combine mashed potatoes (they can be leftover mashed potatoes or instant mashed potatoes, prepared according to package directions) and lard and beaten eggs. Mix well. Add potato mixture to yeast mixture in flour well and mix until smooth. With a large wooden spoon, start working in flour. Let rise until doubled in size.

Roll out to ½ inch thick. Cut with a biscuit cutter. Place on a greased baking sheet and let rise until doubled. Bake at 350°F for 12 minutes. Brush tops with butter and lay waxed paper over top to soften tops. Cover with a cloth until cool.

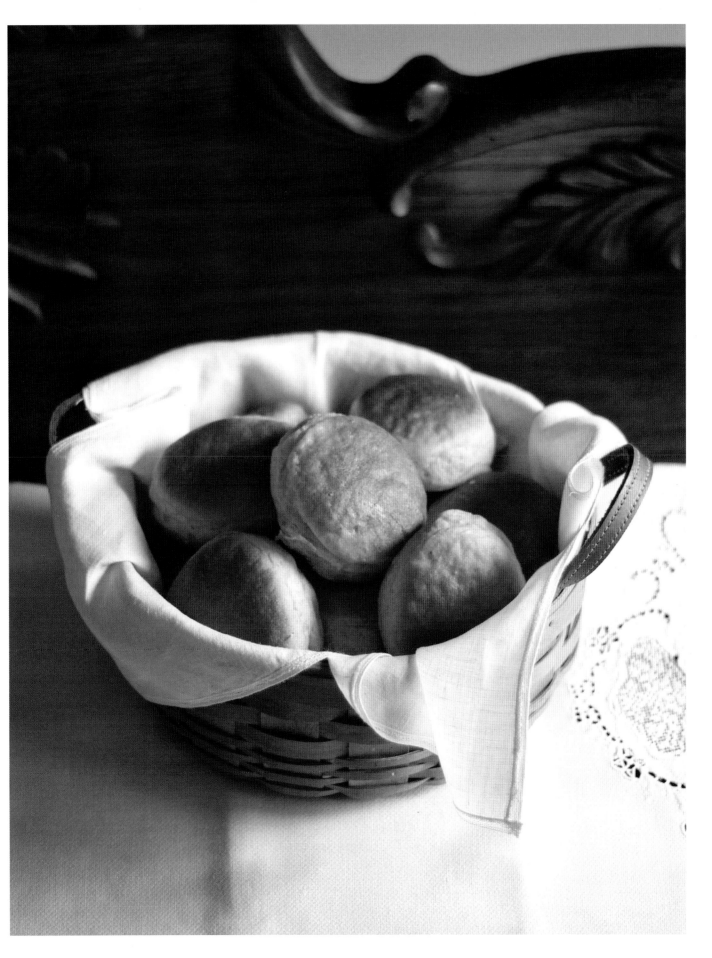

How to plan a meal for guests

I understand that having company is not everyone's cup of tea, but I love to have guests over for a meal. For me, the hardest part of having company for a meal is deciding what to make. I usually ask my husband what he thinks I should make—and then make something totally different. I'm not sure why I even ask the poor man.

I usually start by deciding what meat to make, and then I build the menu around it. In the summer I always seem to plan a grilled meat because it's easy and one mess fewer in the kitchen. I often fix grilled pork chops or grilled chicken. You can buy a whole pork loin and cut it into boneless pork chops for a more economical route.

Once the meat is planned, I start thinking about a hot starch. Roasted potatoes pair nicely with grilled meats. Roasted sweet potatoes are a favorite of mine, and they add color to your table. Some meats, like poor man's steak or country fried pork chops, simply beg for mashed potatoes to be by their side.

A hot vegetable comes next. Will it be green beans, peas, broccoli, limas, or corn? If my meat doesn't have a sauce or gravy, I often make a creamed vegetable. If it does, I will make a simple vegetable like Honey Green Beans (p. 116) or Roasted Broccoli (p. 125).

Now on to a cold salad. If it's summertime, I will use whatever my garden is producing. Cucumber salad, coleslaw, broccoli salad, or lettuce salad. I have quite a few dressing options, but I will often make Poppy Seed Dressing, Balsamic Vinaigrette, Ranch Dressing, or Honey Mustard Dressing for company (see pp. 90–93). Sometimes it's fun to pass around two homemade dressings so my guests can choose.

I usually make desserts using a fruit that is in season. I like to make pies, since they are pretty to look at and easy to serve. If I am in a hurry I will make Cobbler Cake (p. 234) or Cream Cheese and Fruit Delight (p. 239).

I always make sweet iced tea to go along with the meal, and I often make French Bread (p. 36).

The more you do something, the easier it becomes. Having had a lot of guests over the years, I have relaxed as a host. At home when we were growing up, we often hosted guests for Sunday lunch. The week before getting ready for guests, we cleaned everything but the attic. Just ask my sisters. Now I know that it was my mom's clever way of getting lots of tasks done!

But you don't need to wash every surface before you have someone over for a meal. A simple home-cooked meal with a fresh bouquet on the table will help your guests overlook the dirty windows.

PRETZEL BUNS

Makes 12 buns

These buns will change the hamburger game. Once you've had them, you can't make grilled hamburgers without making pretzel buns. Time is one of the most important ingredients in this recipe. Five minutes can make a big difference. Once completely cooled, these rolls are dense. These buns do not keep well, so be sure to eat them fresh!

1½ cup warm water

1 tablespoon active dry yeast

⅓ cup brown sugar

¼ teaspoon salt

4 cups unbleached white flour

2 cups hot water

2 tablespoons baking soda

pretzel salt, for sprinkling

melted butter, for brushing tops

Using a stand mixer fitted with the dough hook, mix together warm water and yeast. Add brown sugar, salt, and flour. Knead on medium speed until dough is smooth and pulls away from the sides of the bowl, around 4–5 minutes. Cover and let rise 10 minutes. Divide dough into 12 even pieces and form into flat 3½-inch round buns. Mix together hot water and baking soda. Dip entire roll into soda mixture. After dipping, place the bun in the palm of your hand and slash the top ⅛ inch deep. Lay on a parchment-lined baking sheet. Sprinkle tops with pretzel salt. Bake at 375°F for 12 minutes. Brush tops with melted butter and serve immediately.

For soft pretzels: This recipe can also be used for soft pretzels. Use ½–¾ cup more flour. The dough cannot be too sticky to roll. After forming pretzels, prepare as directed for buns.

CHEESY BREADSTICKS

Serves 4

I've made this recipe many times for a Sunday evening snack for company. No one will turn down cheesy breadsticks!

1 cup warm water

1 tablespoon active dry yeast

1 tablespoon olive oil

1 tablespoon honey

2½ cups unbleached white flour

1 teaspoon salt

¼ teaspoon garlic powder

¼ teaspoon dried basil

¼ teaspoon dried oregano

⅛ teaspoon salt

several dashes pepper

2 tablespoons butter, melted

½ cup shredded mozzarella cheese

¼ cup freshly grated Parmesan cheese

1 pint (2 cups) pizza sauce (pg. 298)

In a 2-cup liquid measuring cup, whisk together warm water, yeast, oil, and honey. In a medium bowl, combine flour and 1 teaspoon salt. Make a well in the middle of the flour and pour in yeast mixture. Mix together with fork until combined. Knead lightly with your hands and form into a smooth ball. Cover and let rise 20 minutes.

Grease a baking sheet and spread dough to within 1–2 inches of the sides of the baking sheet. In a small bowl, mix together garlic powder, dried basil, dried oregano, ⅛ teaspoon salt, and pepper. Brush dough with melted butter and sprinkle with seasonings mixture. Top with cheeses.

Let rise 15 minutes. Bake at 400°F for 15 minutes. With a pizza cutter, cut into breadsticks and serve warm with pizza sauce.

SOUPS

There is something comforting about warm soup on a cold day. It warms you to your core. In fact, it's hard not to label every winter day a "soup day"!

Soups can be considered a cook's "easy way out," since making soup can mean dumping leftovers in a pot and adding broth or milk. Yet there actually can be lots of love put into a pot of hearty, steaming soup, even one made from leftovers. Quality ingredients and spices can make a pot of soup really sing; when it's paired with homemade bread, you'll hear a harmonious chorus.

We like hearty soups with lots of meat and vegetables. If you find my soups too "hearty," just add more of the liquid the soup calls for; just be sure to adjust the salt. From the vegetable beef soup made from slow-roasted beef to the chicken noodle soup crafted from chicken broth made by simmering chicken bones for hours, nourishment awaits!

Bacon Corn Chowder

Taco Corn Soup

Zuppa Toscana

Hearty Chili

Vegetable Beef Soup

Old-Fashioned Country Ham Potpie

Chicken and Dumpling Soup

Nourishing Chicken Noodle Soup

Chicken Tortilla Soup

Creamy White Chili

BACON CORN CHOWDER

Serves 4

This remains one of Joshua's favorite soups. There is something special about pairing bacon and corn.

---

6 slices bacon, chopped

1 large potato, diced (about 2 cups)

½ onion, diced

¼ cup white cooking wine

1 pint (about 2 cups) frozen corn, thawed

2 tablespoons butter

4 cups milk

2 tablespoons unbleached white flour

½ teaspoon salt

½ teaspoon pepper

½ teaspoon dried parsley flakes

In a soup pot, fry bacon until almost done. Drain off excess bacon grease. Add diced potatoes and onions and fry until bacon is done and onions are translucent.

Add wine to deglaze pot. Stir until nothing is sticking to the bottom of the pot. Add corn and butter, cooking until butter is melted.

In a 4-cup liquid measuring cup, whisk together milk and flour until smooth and pour into pot. Add salt, pepper, and parsley flakes. Simmer on low heat for 10–15 minutes.

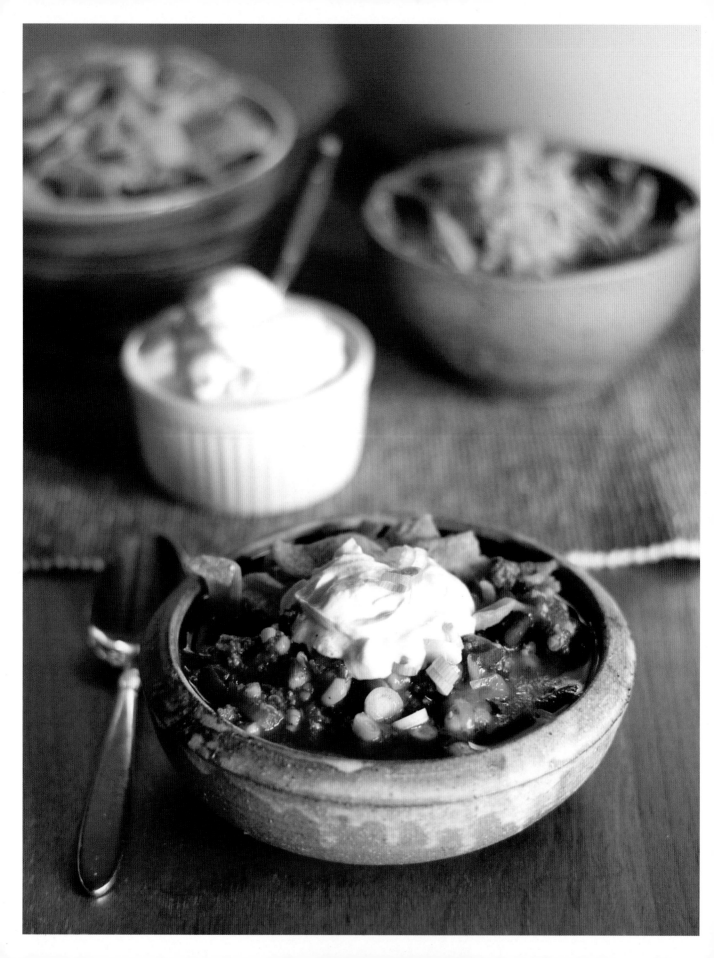

TACO CORN SOUP

Serves 6

I get nostalgic when I make taco corn soup. It's one meal I remember my dad making for supper when we were kids. And in case you wonder, the seasoned salt I use in many recipes is Lawry's.

1 pound ground beef

1 onion, chopped

1 pint (or about 2 cups) frozen corn, thawed

1 (15½-ounce) can black beans, drained

1 (15½-ounce) can Great Northern beans, drained

1 (28-ounce) can diced tomatoes

1 quart (4 cups) tomato juice

1 tablespoon brown sugar

3 tablespoons Taco Seasoning (p. 302)

1 teaspoon chili powder

½ teaspoon seasoned salt

½ teaspoon salt

½ teaspoon pepper

For serving

corn chips

2 cups shredded cheddar cheese

1 cup sour cream

In a soup pot, brown ground beef and onion. Add remaining ingredients and simmer for 20–30 minutes.

Serve with corn chips, shredded cheese, and plenty of sour cream.

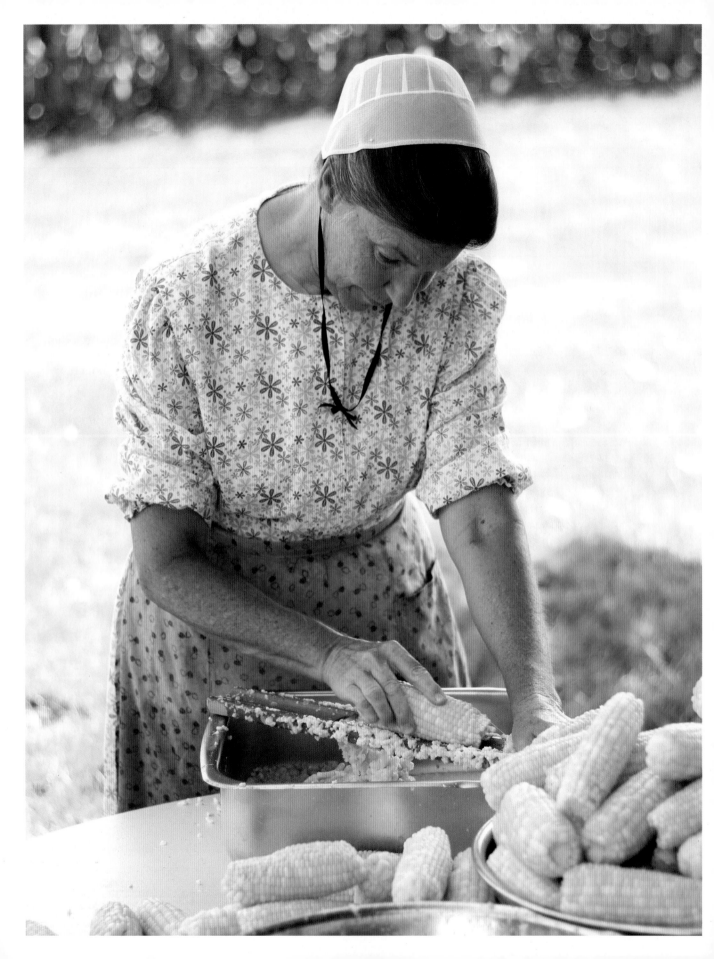

Corn day

Each summer, Dad plants a sweet corn patch along his rows of field corn so we have plenty of corn to work for the freezer. We work our corn on my dad's farm lot, under some shade trees that are close to the dairy parlor. That way we have cold water to cool the corn. It's so nice to work outside and leave the mess out there rather than in a kitchen!

Our corn days start early in the morning, with Dad pulling the sweet corn ears and loading them in a wagon. Our job starts with shucking the ears and blanching them for three minutes. We then cool the corn in tubs of cold water and pick off all the silk before cutting the kernels off. We cut off the kernels with a special corn cutter so that we get creamed corn.

Creamed corn often gets confused with whole-kernel corn that's been thickened with cream. But *real* creamed corn is simply corn that has been cut off the cob with a special cutter. The cutter splits each corn kernel in such a way that the milk from inside the split kernel creates a milky, creamy texture.

We quickly bag the creamed corn, and then Mom runs the creamed corn out the farm lane to the freezer. It's important to get corn chilled and in the freezer quickly, because the sugars turn to starch after the corn has been picked.

I use creamed corn in soups in the winter and also just cook it plain to serve as a side dish. All it needs is a little butter and salt. Some frozen vegetables can be purchased from the grocery store and taste about the same as homegrown. But I have never found any store-bought frozen corn that comes anywhere close to homegrown creamed corn.

ZUPPA TOSCANA

Serves 4

This is a classic Italian soup, and it's a good way to introduce your family to kale. They will love it.

---

1 pound ground pork sausage

¼ teaspoon red pepper flakes

4 slices bacon, chopped

1 large onion, diced

4 garlic cloves, crushed

4 cups chicken stock

6 small red potatoes, cut into half-moon slices

salt and pepper

½ bunch kale, stemmed and chopped (about 8 cups)

1 cup heavy cream

In a soup pot, brown sausage with red pepper flakes. Remove sausage from pot. Add bacon, and fry until crispy. Drain off excess grease. Add onion and sauté until translucent. Add garlic and sauté 1–2 minutes more. Add chicken stock to deglaze pot. Add potatoes, and return browned sausage to pot. Simmer on medium heat until potatoes are fork tender.

Season to taste with salt and pepper. Add kale and cover. Cook just until the kale has wilted. Add heavy cream, stir, and remove from heat.

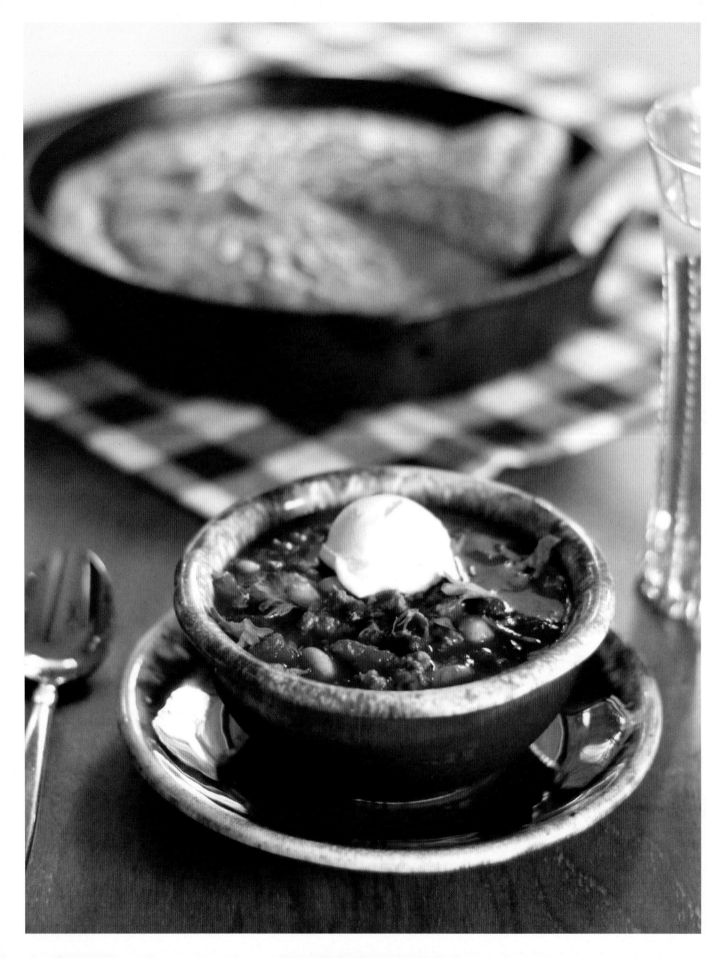

HEARTY CHILI

Serves 6

This is the first soup I think about making in the fall. Be sure to make Aunt Shirley's Corn Bread (p. 32) to go along with it.

1 pound ground beef

1 onion, chopped

1 bell pepper, chopped

2 garlic cloves, crushed

1 (28-ounce) can diced tomatoes

1 (15½-ounce) can black beans, drained

1 (15½-ounce) can Great Northern beans, drained

1 quart (4 cups) tomato juice

¼ cup strong coffee

1 tablespoon white vinegar

1 tablespoon brown sugar

2 teaspoons chili powder

1 teaspoon salt

½ teaspoon seasoned salt

½ teaspoon black pepper

½ teaspoon ground cumin

¼ teaspoon paprika

¼ teaspoon dried oregano

⅛ teaspoon cayenne pepper

In a soup pot, brown ground beef. Add onion and bell pepper and sauté until soft. Add garlic and sauté 2 minutes more. Add remaining ingredients. Simmer on low heat for at least 1 hour.

Serve with sour cream.

VEGETABLE BEEF SOUP

Serves 6–8

This is a great way to use leftover roast beef. It's also the way to a man's heart—at least my husband's.

1 pound ground beef or leftover roast beef

2 teaspoons Better Than Bouillon beef base

2 cups hot water

1 quart (4 cups) tomato juice

1 (28-ounce) can diced tomatoes

2 cups frozen green beans, thawed

½ cup chopped carrots

4 medium potatoes, cubed

1 medium onion, chopped

2 stalks celery, chopped

2 teaspoons Worcestershire sauce

1½ tablespoon brown sugar

1½ teaspoon salt

1 teaspoon seasoned salt

1 teaspoon chili powder

½ teaspoon pepper

½ teaspoon dried basil

½ teaspoon dried oregano

3 tablespoons cornstarch, dissolved in ¼ cup cold water

If using ground beef, brown beef in large soup pot. If using roast beef, cut into pieces and place in pot. Dissolve beef base in hot water. Add broth to pot, along with tomato juice, vegetables, and seasonings. (Do not add cornstarch.) Simmer for 30–40 minutes until vegetables are tender and flavors are set. Stir in dissolved cornstarch and simmer until thickened.

OLD-FASHIONED COUNTRY HAM POTPIE

Serves 4

If you happen to be eating ham for a holiday meal, save the ham bone so you can make some ham potpie. It will comfort your soul.

1 large ham bone

1 cup diced ham

1 cup half-and-half

salt and pepper

Potpie dough

2 cups unbleached white flour

½ teaspoon salt

1 cup water

Place ham bone in a slow cooker and cover with water. Cook on low for 12–18 hours. Strain broth and skim off fat. Transfer the broth to a soup pot and add ham. Simmer broth on low while you make the potpie dough.

Make dough: In small mixing bowl, mix together flour, salt, and water. Add more flour if too sticky. It will be a soft dough. Dust the counter well with flour and roll out dough as thin as possible. With a pizza cutter, cut into 2-inch squares and drop one by one into simmering broth. Cover and simmer 10 minutes. Add half-and-half. Season to taste with salt and freshly ground black pepper.

CHICKEN AND DUMPLING SOUP

Serves 6

When cold weather hits, this soup appears on our supper table. These soft dumplings, covered in a creamy soup base, will keep everyone coming back for more.

8 chicken thighs

2 tablespoons butter

1 teaspoon seasoned salt

½ teaspoon pepper

1 cup chopped carrots

½ cup chopped celery

1 medium onion, thinly sliced

1 pint (about 2 cups) frozen peas, thawed

5 cups chicken stock

1 cup half-and-half

½ cup unbleached white flour

½ teaspoon salt

½ teaspoon pepper

Dumplings

2 cups unbleached white flour

4 teaspoons baking powder

½ teaspoon baking soda

1½ teaspoon salt

¼ teaspoon pepper

6 tablespoons cold butter, grated

1¼ cup buttermilk

Cut chicken thighs into 1-inch pieces. In a soup pot, melt 2 tablespoons butter, add chicken, and sprinkle with seasoned salt and ½ teaspoon pepper. Cook until no longer pink and starting to brown. Add carrots, celery, and onions. Cook until carrots are tender. Add peas. Pour in chicken stock. In a 2-cup liquid measuring cup, whisk together half-and-half and flour until smooth. Pour half-and-half mixture into soup pot while stirring soup. Add salt and ½ teaspoon pepper. Simmer on low.

Make dumplings: In a medium mixing bowl, mix together flour, baking powder, baking soda, salt, and pepper. Add grated butter and mix well. Add buttermilk and stir just until dough comes together. Drop tablespoonfuls into simmering soup and cover. Simmer 10–15 minutes, or until dumplings are firm. (Don't drop more than a tablespoon per dumpling—they will take much longer to cook.)

NOURISHING CHICKEN NOODLE SOUP

Serves 6

This is my go-to soup when anyone in our family is sick. It's important to use bone broth because of the nutrients it adds. I make my bone broth in my electric pressure canner. Simply cover your leftover roasted chicken bones in water and add a little vinegar (which helps to leach out the minerals in the bones). Cook on high pressure for two hours. Strain and use. This makes a nice gelatinous bone broth.

4 boneless, skinless chicken thighs

2 tablespoons butter

salt and pepper

1½ cup chopped carrots

1 cup chopped celery

½ onion, diced

1 large garlic clove, crushed

8 cups chicken bone broth

8 ounces wide uncooked egg noodles

1 teaspoon dried parsley flakes

1 teaspoon salt

freshly ground pepper

Cut chicken thighs into 1-inch pieces. In a soup pot, melt butter and add chicken. Sprinkle with salt and pepper as desired. Fry until golden brown. Add carrots, celery, and onion and sauté until tender. Add garlic, bone broth, uncooked egg noodles, parsley flakes, and 1 teaspoon salt and simmer for 30 minutes. Season to taste with salt and freshly ground pepper.

CHICKEN TORTILLA SOUP

Serves 4

The toppings on this soup make it so delightful. You may find yourself eating handfuls of fried tortilla strips—they are just that good.

---

2 tablespoons butter

½ teaspoon ground cumin

½ teaspoon chili powder

¼ teaspoon salt

¼ teaspoon pepper

4 boneless, skinless chicken thighs

½ onion, chopped

1 jalapeño pepper, seeded and diced

2 large garlic cloves, crushed

4 cups chicken stock

1 (14½-ounce) can diced tomatoes

1 (15-ounce) can black beans, rinsed and drained

¼ cup tomato paste

½ teaspoon sugar

½ teaspoon chili powder

½ teaspoon salt

freshly ground pepper, as desired

Toppings

3 tortillas, cut into ½-inch strips

1 cup sour cream

2 cups shredded cheddar cheese

2 avocados, chopped and tossed in lemon juice

½ cup chopped cilantro

Melt butter in soup pot. Mix together cumin, ½ teaspoon chili powder, ¼ teaspoon salt, and pepper and sprinkle on both sides of chicken thighs. Fry chicken on medium-high heat, flipping after 3–4 minutes. Fry until golden brown. Remove from pot and shred with two forks. Set aside.

Add onion, jalapeño pepper, and garlic to the soup pot drippings; sauté until soft. Add shredded chicken, chicken stock, tomatoes, beans, tomato paste, sugar, ½ teaspoon chili powder, and ½ teaspoon salt. Grind in fresh pepper. Simmer 20–30 minutes so flavors can blend.

While soup is simmering, heat ½ inch oil in a skillet. Add tortilla strips and fry until crispy. Drain on paper towel.

Serve soup hot with tortilla strips and other toppings of your choice.

CREAMY WHITE CHILI

Serves 6

This is a hearty and creamy chili with a little kick of spice.

---

3 boneless, skinless chicken breasts

1 tablespoon canola oil

1 medium onion, chopped

4 garlic cloves, crushed

4 cups chicken stock

2 (15½-ounce) cans Great Northern beans, rinsed and drained

2 (4-ounce) cans green chilies, chopped

1 teaspoon ground cumin

1 teaspoon dried oregano

¼ teaspoon cayenne pepper

1 teaspoon salt

½ teaspoon pepper

1 cup sour cream

½ cup heavy cream

Cut chicken into 1-inch pieces. In a soup pot, heat oil, and add chicken, onion, and garlic. Sauté until chicken is no longer pink. Add chicken stock, beans, chilies, cumin, oregano, cayenne pepper, salt, and pepper. Bring to boil. Reduce heat and simmer for 30 minutes. Remove from heat and stir in sour cream and heavy cream.

SALADS, DRESSINGS, AND SAUCES

I always serve a green salad with our meals. Salads have a way of rounding out meals and adding nutrition and color too. I try to always keep one homemade dressing in the refrigerator so it can quickly be used for making a salad. Keeping too many dressings on hand at one time can cause confusion about which one is still fresh and can lead to waste in the end.

Homemade sauces and dressings have a way of making foods seem extra special. Imagine dipping hot and crispy sweet potato fries in a tiny bowl of homemade Southwest Dipping Sauce (p. 95). It creates a feeling I just really can't explain. Maybe that old saying is really true: the secret is in the sauce!

Fresh Berry Medley	Poppy Seed Dressing
Festive Cranberry Salad	Celery Seed Dressing
Crunchy Broccoli Salad	Balsamic Vinaigrette
Oil and Vinegar Pasta Salad	Blue Cheese Dressing
Dad's Favorite Potato Salad	Ranch Dressing
Fresh Garden Salsa	Honey Mustard Dressing
Creamy Coleslaw	Tartar Sauce
Cold Taco Salad	Creamy Horseradish Sauce
Chicken Salad	French Fry Sauce
Grandma's Pickled Eggs	Cocktail Sauce
Classic Creamy Dressing	Southwest Dipping Sauce

FRESH BERRY MEDLEY

Serves 8–10

This recipe came from my sister-in-law, Nadya. I love how light and fresh the lemon zest makes it.

1 cup sparkling wine or white grape juice

½ cup sugar

⅛ teaspoon salt

1½ teaspoon lemon zest

1 tablespoon lemon juice

½ teaspoon vanilla extract

8 cups mixed fresh berries (strawberries, raspberries, and blueberries)

In a small saucepan, combine all ingredients except the fruit. Heat to boiling. Refrigerate.

In medium bowl, toss fruit with chilled sauce. Refrigerate 1–2 more hours before serving. Garnish with fresh mint, if desired.

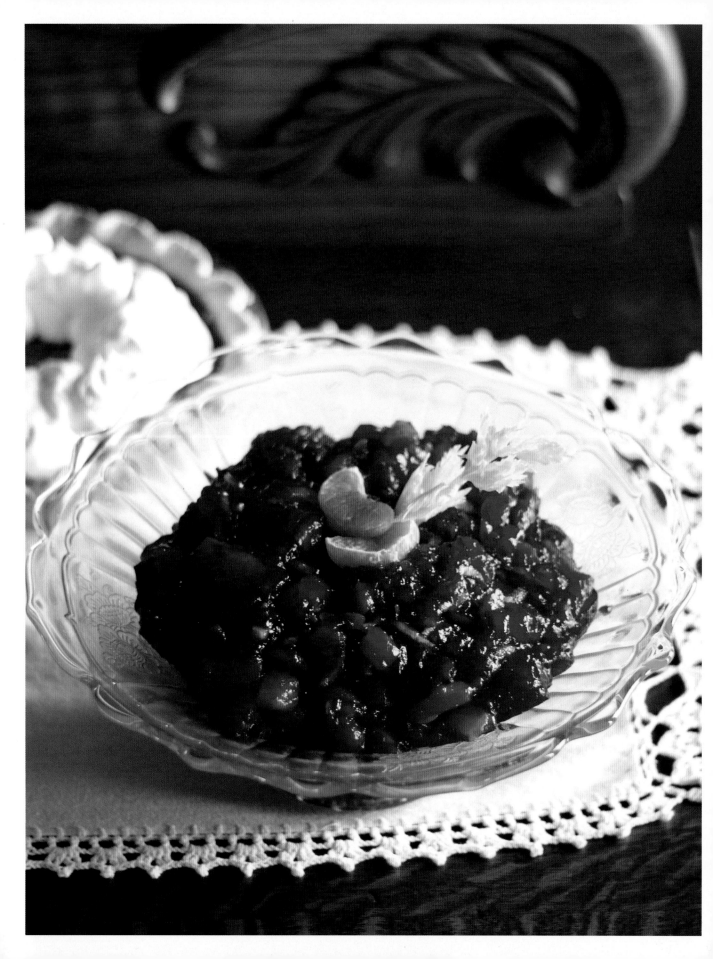

FESTIVE CRANBERRY SALAD

Serves 30

This is my grandma Shank's recipe. It makes a lot, so it's a great dish for large family gatherings at Thanksgiving or Christmas. It just wouldn't be Thanksgiving without Grandma's cranberry salad!

1 (12-ounce) bag fresh cranberries

1 cup sugar

1 cup water

3 (3-ounce) boxes raspberry gelatin

2 cups hot water

3 cups cold water

6 apples, grated

4 oranges, cubed

1 (20-ounce) can crushed pineapple, do not drain

½ cup finely chopped celery

In a small saucepan, cook cranberries, sugar, and 1 cup water until cranberries pop open and mixture thickens slightly.

In a large bowl, dissolve raspberry gelatin in 2 cups hot water. Add 3 cups cold water. Add cooked cranberry mixture and mix well. Chill until starting to gel (this helps the fruit not to soak up the gelatin color) then fold in apples, oranges, pineapple, and celery.

Refrigerate overnight until gelled.

NOTE: Do not use fresh pineapple! Your gelatin will not gel.

CRUNCHY BROCCOLI SALAD

Serves 6–8

This is a colorful salad packed with color and flavor. A great way to enjoy fresh broccoli from your garden.

6–8 cups chopped broccoli

⅔ cup dried cranberries

½ cup chopped spring onions

½ cup chopped pecans

Dressing

1 cup mayonnaise

3 tablespoons white vinegar

⅓ cup sugar

¼ teaspoon salt

In a medium bowl, toss together broccoli, dried cranberries, spring onions, and pecans. In a liquid 2-cup measuring cup, whisk together dressing ingredients. Pour desired amount of dressing over salad and toss just before serving.

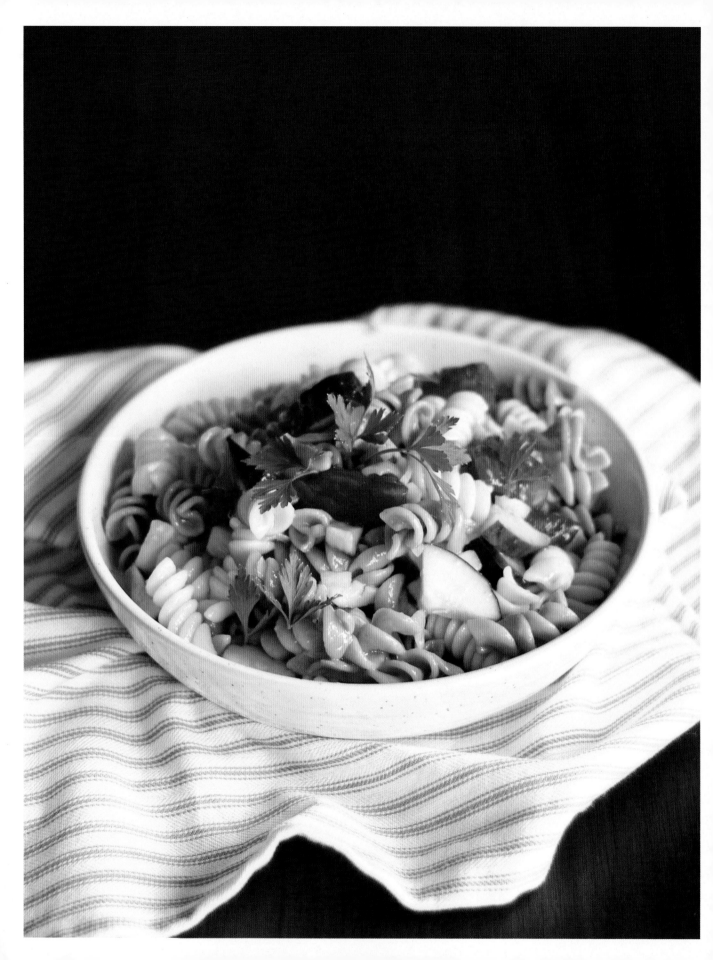

OIL AND VINEGAR PASTA SALAD

Serves 8

This pasta salad is a great addition to summer picnics. It's also a great way to use fresh garden vegetables. Use the vegetables listed simply as a guide; I usually use whatever vegetables I have on hand.

3 cups uncooked tricolor rotini pasta

1 teaspoon salt

2 cups chopped cucumbers

1 cup chopped tomatoes

¼ red onion, chopped

Dressing

1 cup oil

¾ cup white vinegar

¾ cup sugar

½ teaspoon salt

In a pot, cook pasta with 1 teaspoon salt according to package directions. Drain.

In a large bowl, whisk together dressing ingredients and add warm pasta. Cover and refrigerate for at least 6 hours. Mix in chopped vegetables 2 hours before serving.

Grape juice

Many Mennonite homes have homemade grape juice on their canning shelves. Pop some popcorn to eat along with grape juice, and you have a traditional Sunday evening snack. If you'd drink and eat the same thing on a Wednesday evening, it wouldn't taste as good as it does on a Sunday evening. Traditions have a way of making you anticipate things—of expecting a rhythm to life.

We have some grapevines in our front yard that Joshua's grandparents planted when they lived here. The white grapes make the best grape juice. Instead of steaming our grapes for juice, we have started to make the juice by canning whole grapes.

To can grape juice: Place 2 cups grapes in a quart jar along with ⅓ cup sugar or a scant ¼ teaspoon stevia. Fill the jar with water up to ½ inch below the neck of the jar, so the jars won't run over when they are processed. Place lids and rings on jars and process in a boiling water bath for 15 minutes. (Canning times are subject to change according to USDA regulations. Check your county extension office or the National Center for Home Food Preservation website.)

Strain out grapes just before serving. We usually just add ice and ginger ale. Grape juice and popcorn are all you need after a large Sunday lunch and an afternoon nap.

DAD'S FAVORITE POTATO SALAD

Serves 10

This recipe comes from my mom. It's a favorite of my dad's. You can bet he will always request it for his birthday meal, along with Pulled Pork Barbecue (p. 161).

2 pounds potatoes

1 tablespoon salt

5 hard-cooked eggs, grated or chopped

½ cup chopped onion

¾ cup diced celery

Dressing

1½ cup mayonnaise

2 tablespoons yellow mustard

3 tablespoons white vinegar

½ cup sugar

1½ teaspoon salt

Peel and halve potatoes and place in a large pot of water. Add salt. Cook just until tender, about 15 minutes. They should pierce easily with a fork but still be firm. Cool quickly in ice water, then grate or dice.

In a medium bowl, whisk together dressing ingredients. Add cooked potatoes, eggs, onion, and celery. Toss well. Refrigerate for 12 hours before serving.

FRESH GARDEN SALSA

Serves 4

A fresh-tasting summer snack that goes well with tortilla chips or tacos, enchiladas, burritos, and even eggs.

2 cups diced and drained fresh tomatoes

1 cup blanched fresh corn kernels

½ green bell pepper, diced

⅓ cup diced onion

1 jalapeño pepper, finely chopped

1 teaspoon chopped fresh cilantro

juice of ½ lemon

¼ teaspoon sugar

½ teaspoon salt

⅛ teaspoon pepper

In a medium bowl, mix together ingredients. Refrigerate 1 hour before serving so flavors can blend.

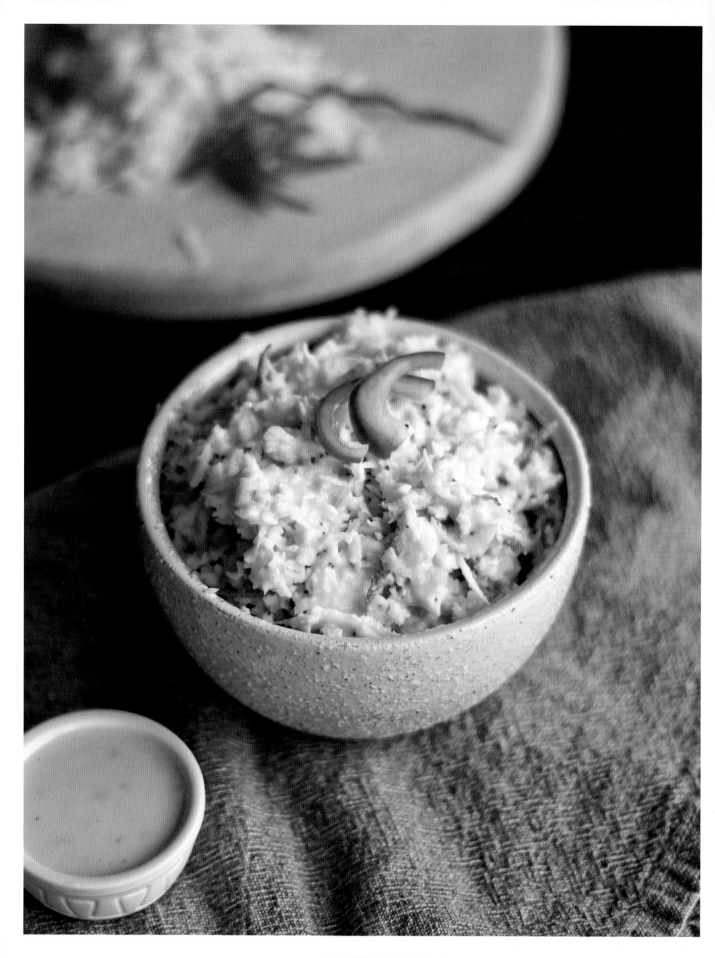

CREAMY COLESLAW

Serves 12

I like a creamy dressing for coleslaw with just enough sweetness and some zip at the end. I often grate a whole head of cabbage in my food processor and mix up the dressing to keep in the refrigerator. Then I have the ingredients on hand so that I can quickly toss together coleslaw for meals all week.

---

1 head cabbage, grated

1 large carrot, peeled and grated

Dressing

½ cup canola oil

½ cup mayonnaise

⅓ cup white vinegar

1 tablespoon yellow mustard

1 small onion, quartered

½ cup sugar

1 teaspoon salt

½ teaspoon celery seed

In a large bowl, toss together cabbage and carrots.

Blend dressing ingredients well in a blender and refrigerate until ready to toss with cabbage and carrots. Toss desired amount of cabbage mixture with dressing right before serving.

COLD TACO SALAD

Serves 6–8

A quick, cool summer meal that tastes great paired with iced mint tea. Taco salad also makes a great packed lunch to take away.

Meat and beans

1 pound ground beef

1 medium onion, chopped

1 (15½-ounce) can black beans, drained

2 tablespoons Taco Seasoning (p. 302)

Dressing

1 cup mayonnaise

¼ cup ketchup

2 tablespoons white vinegar

1 teaspoon yellow mustard

¼ cup sugar

½ teaspoon paprika

¼ teaspoon salt

Salad

1 large head romaine lettuce, chopped

3 tomatoes, chopped

1 large cucumber, sliced

2 cups shredded cheddar cheese

small bag of corn chips, crushed

2 (2¼-ounce) cans sliced black olives

In a skillet, brown ground beef with onion. Add beans and taco seasoning. Stir. Remove from heat and allow to cool.

In a 2-cup liquid measuring cup, whisk together dressing ingredients.

In a large mixing bowl, add meat-and-beans mixture, lettuce, tomato, cucumber, cheese, crushed chips, and olives. Toss with enough dressing to coat evenly. Serve immediately.

CHICKEN SALAD

Serves 4

A quick way to make a tasty lunch with leftover chicken. I love to use my Sweet Dill Pickles (p. 294) in this.

½ cup mayonnaise

1 tablespoon honey

2 teaspoons white vinegar

1 teaspoon Dijon mustard

½ teaspoon seasoned salt

½ teaspoon pepper

2 cups chopped cooked chicken

⅓ cup chopped sweet dill pickles

4 hard-cooked eggs, diced

1 stalk celery, chopped

2 tablespoons diced onion

In a medium bowl, mix together mayonnaise, honey, vinegar, and mustard; add seasoned salt and pepper. Fold in chicken, pickles, eggs, celery, and onion. Refrigerate for 30 minutes before serving. Serve on bread, crackers, or lettuce leaves.

GRANDMA'S PICKLED EGGS

Makes 18 eggs

Grandma used to make pickled eggs every Easter. Now that she's older she can't do that any-more. But I'm so thankful to have her recipe.

18 eggs

Syrup

1 cup beet juice (drain from 1 pint pickled beets)

1 cup sugar

1 cup white vinegar

1 teaspoon salt

Carefully place eggs in a large pot and cover with water. Bring to a hard boil. Remove from heat, cover, and let stand for 12 minutes. Remove from pot and add to a bowl of ice water. Peel and place in a half-gallon jar.

Drain the juice off the pickled beets. If you don't have a full cup, add water to the beets and shake the jar a bit to get more juice. In a small saucepan, mix together beet juice, sugar, vinegar, and salt. Bring to a boil. Pour hot syrup over eggs and refrigerate. Shake the jar a couple of times a day so the eggs are pickled evenly. After 3 days the eggs are ready to eat and will keep up to a month.

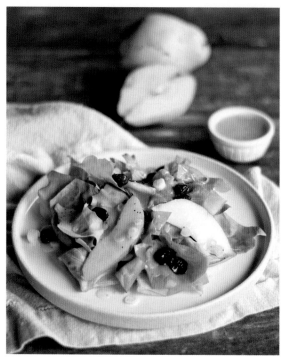

CLASSIC CREAMY DRESSING

Makes about 3 cups

I use this dressing on cucumber salads, fresh garden salads, thinly sliced cabbage, and watercress. For a different twist you can use lime juice instead of vinegar. The lime juice version pairs well with cabbage.

2 cups mayonnaise

⅓ cup milk

3 tablespoons white vinegar

⅓ cup sugar

½ teaspoon salt

In a small bowl, whisk together ingredients. Serve on the side with a salad or toss right before serving.

POPPY SEED DRESSING

Makes about 1 cup

This dressing is delightful drizzled on a leafy lettuce salad garnished with pears or strawberries. If the dressing separates after being chilled, vigorously shake the dressing in a jar with a tightly closed lid. It will emulsify again.

½ cup canola oil

3 tablespoons white vinegar

1 teaspoon yellow mustard

¼ cup chopped onion

⅓ cup sugar

½ teaspoon salt

½ teaspoon poppy seeds

Place all ingredients except poppy seeds in a blender and blend well. Stir in poppy seeds.

CELERY SEED DRESSING

Makes about 2 cups

This recipe has been a part of my family for years! If the dressing separates after being chilled, vigorously shake the dressing in a jar with a tightly closed lid. It will emulsify again.

---

1 cup canola oil

⅓ cup white vinegar

1½ teaspoon yellow mustard

¼ cup chopped onion

⅔ cup sugar

1 teaspoon salt

1 teaspoon celery seeds

Place all ingredients in a blender and blend well. Refrigerate until ready to serve.

BALSAMIC VINAIGRETTE

Makes about 1 cup

A classic vinaigrette with great flavor. If the dressing separates after being chilled, vigorously shake the dressing in a jar with a tightly closed lid. It will emulsify again.

½ cup olive oil

¼ cup honey

¼ cup balsamic vinegar

1 tablespoon Dijon mustard

⅛ teaspoon salt

freshly ground pepper, to taste

Pour all ingredients into a pint jar and shake well.

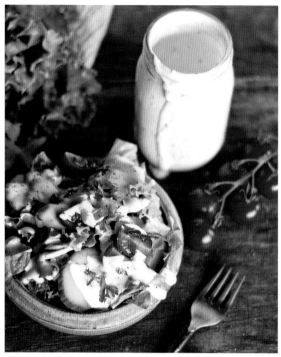

BLUE CHEESE DRESSING

Makes about 2 cups

A great dressing for all those blue cheese lovers!

1 cup mayonnaise

½ cup sour cream

½ cup milk

2 tablespoons white vinegar

¼ cup blue cheese crumbles

1 teaspoon parsley flakes

1 teaspoon sugar

¼ teaspoon dry mustard

¼ teaspoon salt

¼ teaspoon pepper

In a small bowl, mix together all ingredients. Refrigerate until ready to serve.

RANCH DRESSING

Makes about 1½ cup

You will find yourself drizzling this dressing over many things. It's that good. We drizzle it over chicken fajitas, taco salad, and green salads. If you don't have fresh parsley on hand, dried parsley flakes will work.

1 garlic clove, crushed

1 teaspoon chopped fresh parsley

1 cup mayonnaise

½ cup buttermilk

1 teaspoon white vinegar

1 teaspoon lemon juice

1 teaspoon sugar

½ teaspoon salt

½ teaspoon black pepper

⅛ teaspoon cayenne pepper

⅛ teaspoon paprika

In a small bowl, mix ingredients together well. Refrigerate until ready to serve.

HONEY MUSTARD DRESSING

Makes about 1½ cup

This can be used as a salad dressing or a dipping sauce. It's delightful as a dip for Crispy Chicken Nuggets (p. 205).

1 cup mayonnaise

⅓ cup honey

2 tablespoons yellow mustard

1 teaspoon white vinegar

dash paprika

dash salt

In a small bowl, mix together ingredients. Refrigerate until ready to serve.

TARTAR SAUCE

Makes about ½ cup

Serve this with Baked Fish (p. 221) or Crab Cakes (p. 227).

¼ cup sour cream

¼ cup mayonnaise

1 tablespoon sweet pickle relish

½ teaspoon lemon juice

¼ teaspoon dried dill weed

In a small bowl, mix together ingredients. Refrigerate until ready to serve.

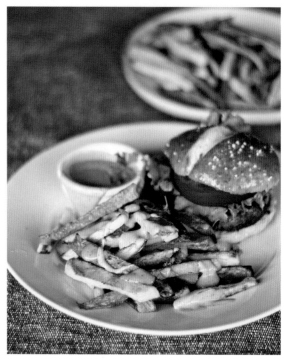

CREAMY HORSERADISH SAUCE

Makes about 1½ cups

This sauce is lovely when paired with roast beef.

½ cup sour cream

½ cup mayonnaise

⅛ cup Dijon mustard

1 tablespoon cream-style horseradish

½ teaspoon lemon juice

½ teaspoon granulated sugar

¼ teaspoon salt

In a small bowl, mix together ingredients well.

FRENCH FRY SAUCE

Makes about 2 cups

A great dipping sauce for crispy french fries.

1 cup mayonnaise

1 cup ketchup

4 teaspoons white vinegar

½ teaspoon pepper

¼ teaspoon salt

¼ teaspoon paprika

⅛ teaspoon cayenne pepper

In a small bowl, mix together ingredients.

COCKTAIL SAUCE

Makes about 1 cup

An easy homemade cocktail sauce that pairs nicely with steamed shrimp.

¾ cup ketchup

1 tablespoon lemon juice

½ teaspoon Worcestershire sauce

2 teaspoons horse-radish sauce

2 teaspoons brown sugar

¼ teaspoon salt

freshly ground pepper, to taste

In a small bowl, mix together ingredients. Refrigerate until ready to serve.

SOUTHWEST DIPPING SAUCE

Makes 1¼ cup

This sauce is delightful with Sweet Potato Fries (p. 110).

1 cup mayonnaise

¼ cup ketchup

1 teaspoon white vinegar

¼ teaspoon paprika

dash salt

In a small bowl, mix together ingredients well. Refrigerate until ready to serve.

Watercress

Every year I look forward to the first greens of spring. In April, watercress is one of the first to come. It grows in the natural cold springs around our town. We head over to a local spring and gather all we want.

You can choose to wear boots (like my mom, who is afraid of something in the water biting her toes), or you can wade barefoot in the icy-cold spring water, like I do, for the full experience. Caroline enjoys tagging along and tramping through the chilly waters while I gather the watercress.

To harvest the watercress, we cut off the tender tops. When we have gathered a nice amount, we head home to wash the watercress several times. A lot of washing is required, because of sand from the spring. Watercress will keep in a bag in the refrigerator for several days.

Watercress is packed with nutrition. According to the Organic Facts website, watercress contains "more vitamin C than an orange, more calcium than milk, more iron than spinach, and more folate than bananas."

I serve watercress as a salad. I add hard-cooked eggs, spring onions, and crispy bacon bits, tossed in my Classic Creamy Dressing (p. 90). Watercress has a bit of a bitter bite at the end, but paired with a creamy dressing and hearty toppings, it is just delightful. Watercress salad can usually be found on the table at my extended Rhodes family Easter gatherings.

VEGETABLES AND SIDE DISHES

Vegetables are the tool to making a colorful meal. My mom always made sure our meals weren't all the same color. Since we grow most of our vegetables, I don't like to add much to them. For meals, I almost always fix a meat, hot starch, hot vegetable, and green salad. If I am making a richer meat (for example, one with gravy or sauce), I don't make a creamy vegetable. I usually fix a roasted vegetable and a colorful salad. If we are having creamed corn as a hot vegetable, I also try to make sweet potatoes to add a pop of color.

Red-Skinned Mashed Potatoes

Brown Butter Potatoes

Cheesy Creamed Potatoes

Rosemary Roasted Potatoes

Baked Sweet Potatoes with Cinnamon Butter

Maple-Glazed Sweet Potatoes

Citrus-Glazed Sweet Potatoes

Parmesan Roasted Sweet Potatoes

Sweet Potato Fries

Creamy Macaroni and Cheese

Slow-Baked Macaroni

Oven-Roasted Green Beans

Honey Green Beans

Grilled Mushrooms

Classic Bread Stuffing

Creamed Lima Beans (or Peas)

Roasted Broccoli

Perfect Broccoli

Stuffed Peppers

Rice and Beans

RED-SKINNED MASHED POTATOES

Serves 12

This recipe can also be used for regular white mashed potatoes. If using Yukon Gold potatoes, add less milk because they contain more moisture. No matter what kind of potatoes you use, don't overmash them. Mashing them releases starch, and too much mashing can make them gluey.

5 pounds red potatoes, scrubbed and quartered

1 teaspoon salt

½ cup butter, softened

1 (8-ounce) package cream cheese

1 cup sour cream

1 cup milk, warmed

2 teaspoons salt

¼ teaspoon onion powder

Place potatoes into a large pot and cover with water. Add 1 teaspoon salt. Cook until you can easily poke through them with a fork (20–25 minutes); drain. Place in a mixing bowl and beat with an electric mixer until smooth. Add softened butter and beat until incorporated. Add cream cheese and sour cream, then add warm milk, ¼ cup at a time, until potatoes are creamy but not runny. Add 2 teaspoons salt and onion powder. Mix well and season to taste with additional salt.

Spread into a greased baking dish and cover with foil. Bake at 350°F for 45 minutes until hot and bubbly. Garnish with melted butter and parsley flakes, if desired.

TIP: Unbaked, these potatoes freeze well. When thawed, the texture will seem different, but once they are baked they are fine.

BROWN BUTTER POTATOES

Serves 6

This is an old recipe that my grandma says her mother taught her how to make. It's a great way to fix new garden potatoes.

3 pounds potatoes, scrubbed and quartered

1 teaspoon salt

½ cup butter

⅔ cup unbleached white flour

¼ cup chopped parsley

½ teaspoon salt

freshly ground pepper

Place potatoes in a large pot and cover with water. Add 1 teaspoon salt. Cook until just tender, or about 20 minutes; drain.

In a large, deep skillet, melt butter. Add flour and stir until smooth and starting to brown. You will start to smell it browning. Add chopped parsley and ½ teaspoon salt. Add cooked potatoes, tossing with brown butter mixture until evenly coated. Sprinkle with freshly ground pepper and garnish with additional fresh parsley, if desired. Serve with sour cream on the side.

CHEESY CREAMED POTATOES

Serves 6

This recipe is a new take on the classic gourmet potatoes that I grew up eating.

1½ pound potatoes

½ cup chopped onion

2 tablespoons butter

2 tablespoons unbleached white flour

1 cup milk

1 teaspoon salt

½ cup sour cream

1½ cup shredded cheddar cheese, divided

½ teaspoon parsley flakes

Peel potatoes and cook until just tender (around 15 minutes). They should pierce easily with a fork but still be firm. Cool quickly in ice water and grate. This should yield about 4 cups grated potatoes.

In a small skillet, sauté onions in a little oil until translucent. Set aside.

In a saucepan, melt butter; add flour and whisk until smooth. Add milk and salt; cook until thickened. Remove from heat and add sour cream, 1 cup shredded cheddar cheese, and parsley flakes. Fold in grated potatoes and sautéed onions. Spoon into a greased 9-inch cast iron skillet or 9-inch baking dish. Sprinkle with remaining ½ cup cheese and garnish with additional parsley flakes. Bake, covered, at 350°F for 30 minutes, then uncover and bake 10 minutes more.

ROSEMARY ROASTED POTATOES

Serves 10

One of my favorite summer meals is grilled chicken, these potatoes, creamed peas, and a garden salad. My aunt Bonnie created this potato recipe for our wedding. It's a favorite of mine—simple yet delicious. I often serve these when I have Sunday company.

3 pounds red potatoes

⅓ cup olive oil

1 tablespoon minced fresh rosemary

1 tablespoon minced fresh chives

1 teaspoon salt

1 teaspoon pepper

¼ teaspoon garlic powder

Cut potatoes into quarters (about 8 cups). In a small bowl, mix together oil and seasonings. In a large bowl, toss oil mixture over potatoes and spread out on a large baking sheet lined with parchment paper. Bake at 425°F for 35 minutes. Serve with sour cream.

BAKED SWEET POTATOES
with Cinnamon Butter
Serves 4–6

I'll eat a baked sweet potato any day of the week. I love them. This cinnamon butter adds a special touch.

4 large sweet potatoes
oil
salt and pepper

Cinnamon butter
½ cup butter, softened
⅓ cup brown sugar
½ teaspoon ground cinnamon
½ teaspoon salt

Clean sweet potatoes well and poke all over with a fork. Rub with oil. Place on a baking sheet lined with parchment paper and bake at 400°F for 45 minutes, or until soft.

In a mixing bowl, beat together cinnamon butter ingredients until smooth. Use a small cookie scoop to scoop butter onto a plate. Refrigerate until set.

Slice open baked sweet potatoes and top with a scoop or two of cinnamon butter. Season to taste with salt and pepper.

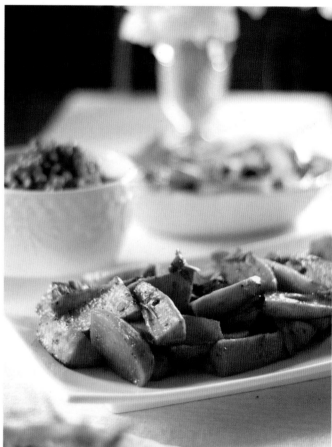

MAPLE-GLAZED SWEET POTATOES

Serves 4–6

This is a simple way to make a tasty side dish. A different twist on the classic candied sweet potatoes made at Thanksgiving.

2 large sweet potatoes

2–3 tablespoons olive oil

maple syrup

salt

Peel sweet potatoes and slice into ¾-inch rounds. Place in a bowl and coat evenly with oil. Lay on a baking sheet lined with parchment paper. Drizzle tops with maple syrup and sprinkle with salt. Bake at 400°F for 30–35 minutes. Flip potatoes halfway through the baking time. This helps to get both sides coated in the maple syrup. The potatoes are done when they are soft but not falling apart.

CITRUS-GLAZED SWEET POTATOES

Serves 4

The lemon juice makes these potatoes vibrant.

2 large sweet potatoes, peeled and cut into wedges (about 6 cups)

juice of ½ lemon

2 tablespoons olive oil

3 tablespoons honey

¾ teaspoon salt

½ teaspoon pepper

¼ teaspoon ground cumin

¼ teaspoon garlic powder

⅛ teaspoon cayenne pepper (optional)

Place sweet potato wedges in a 9 x 13-inch baking dish lined with parchment paper. In a small bowl, mix together remaining ingredients. Drizzle glaze over potatoes and toss with hands until evenly coated. Bake at 425°F for 30 minutes, stirring halfway through.

PARMESAN ROASTED SWEET POTATOES

Serves 4

There is something special about tiny cubes of sweet potatoes. Maybe it's because you know someone took the time to cut them, and you can feel the love that's been poured into them. You could also use half white potatoes for a colorful twist.

---

3 medium sweet potatoes, peeled and cubed (about 5 cups)

2 tablespoons butter, melted

1 tablespoon olive oil

1 large garlic clove, minced or crushed

½ teaspoon salt

¼ cup freshly grated Parmesan cheese

Place potatoes in a 9 x 13-inch baking dish lined with parchment paper. In a small bowl, mix together butter, oil, garlic, and salt. Drizzle butter mixture over potatoes and toss with hands until evenly coated. Sprinkle with cheese. Bake at 425°F for 20 minutes, or until soft and slightly brown. Garnish with parsley flakes and freshly ground pepper, if desired. Taste for salt and sprinkle on more if needed.

SWEET POTATO FRIES

Serves 4

It's amazing how many sweet potatoes you can eat when they are cut into fries! The cornstarch in this recipe makes them crispier.

---

4 large sweet potatoes (about 2 pounds), peeled and cut into ½-inch fries

2 tablespoons canola oil

1 tablespoon cornstarch

1 teaspoon salt

1 teaspoon seasoned salt

1 teaspoon garlic powder

½ teaspoon pepper

¼ teaspoon ground cumin

⅛ teaspoon cayenne pepper (optional)

Place fries in a gallon-sized resealable plastic bag. Add canola oil, close bag, and flip bag over and over until fries are evenly coated in oil.

In a small bowl, mix together remaining ingredients and sprinkle into bag. Repeat flipping process until fries are evenly coated with seasoning mixture. Evenly space fries on two baking sheets lined with parchment paper. (Make sure fries aren't touching. If they are too close together, they will steam instead of roast, resulting in soggy fries.) Bake at 425°F for 30 minutes, flipping the fries halfway through. Oven times may vary; just bake until the fries are soft inside and crispy on the outside. Dip in Southwest Dipping Sauce (p. 95).

CREAMY MACARONI AND CHEESE

Serves 6

I've made this recipe for years. Making a white sauce with milk gives this macaroni a wonderful texture. If you are a processed cheese fan, go ahead and use it! You may just need to cut back on the salt.

2 cups uncooked elbow macaroni

1 tablespoon butter

½ teaspoon salt

Sauce

¼ cup butter

2 tablespoons unbleached white flour

3 cups milk

1 teaspoon Dijon mustard

1 heaping teaspoon salt

½ teaspoon pepper

1 cup shredded mild cheddar cheese

1 cup shredded Monterey Jack or Gouda cheese

½ cup additional shredded cheese

In a medium saucepan, boil macaroni with butter and salt, or according to package directions, until just done (about 8 minutes). Drain and set aside.

Make sauce: In a saucepan using low heat, melt butter and then add flour, whisking until smooth. Cook 1 minute. Add milk, Dijon mustard, salt, and pepper. Heat on low until slightly thickened. Do not boil. Remove from heat and add cheddar cheese and Monterey Jack or Gouda cheese. Stir until melted.

Add macaroni to sauce and then pour into a greased baking dish. (I like to use my 10-inch cast iron skillet; but a 9 x 13-inch dish also works.) Sprinkle with ½ cup shredded cheese. Bake at 350°F for 15–20 minutes until bubbling hot and the cheese on top melts. The sauce should thicken but remain creamy; it will set up as it cools on the table.

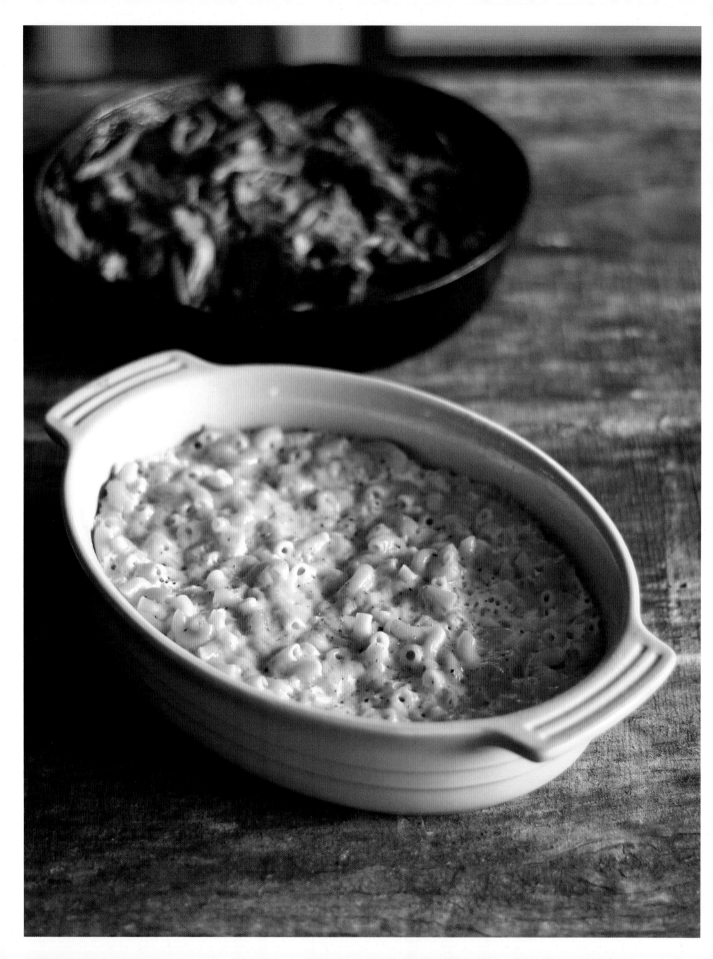

SLOW-BAKED MACARONI

Serves 6

A quick side dish for Sunday lunch that can be ready the moment you walk in the door from church.

2 cups uncooked elbow macaroni

2 tablespoons butter, melted

2 teaspoons salt

2 cups shredded cheese (I use Gouda and cheddar)

4½ cups milk

In a 9 x 13-inch baking dish, mix together macaroni, butter, and salt. Add cheese and mix until evenly combined. Pour milk over top. Bake, covered, at 235°F for 3 hours.

OVEN-ROASTED GREEN BEANS

Serves 4

Roasting green beans in the oven enhances their flavor. I used to can all my green beans, but now I freeze them all and roast them in the oven. The texture and color surpass canned green beans.

1 quart (about 4 cups) frozen green beans, thawed

1 teaspoon salt

¼ cup water

1 small onion, sliced

3 slices bacon

2 teaspoons brown sugar

Place green beans in a buttered 9 x 9-inch baking dish or cast iron skillet. Sprinkle with salt and toss with hands to coat evenly. Add water to help keep moist while roasting. Sprinkle onions over beans. With kitchen scissors, snip bacon pieces evenly over top. Sprinkle with brown sugar. Bake at 375°F for 45 minutes.

TIP: If using canned green beans, use only ¼ teaspoon salt and bake 30 minutes.

HONEY GREEN BEANS

Serves 4

I've made these green beans for weddings and banquets. A different twist on the classic green bean. The honey makes them special.

2 tablespoons bacon grease or butter

¼ onion, sliced

4 cups frozen, uncut green beans

2 tablespoons honey

1 teaspoon salt

In a large skillet, melt bacon grease or butter and add onions. Sauté onions until translucent. Add green beans; drizzle with honey and sprinkle with salt. Cover and cook 10 minutes, or until slightly crunchy. Uncover and simmer on high for a few minutes to reduce the liquid in the pan.

GRILLED MUSHROOMS

Serves 6

A great summer side dish when you are grilling. I prefer these over candy—they are that good!

1 pound fresh mushrooms

¼ cup butter

2 garlic cloves, crushed

½ teaspoon salt

½ teaspoon pepper

½ teaspoon parsley flakes

Use a dry brush to clean mushrooms. (Do not wash or they will get soggy.) Cut large mushrooms in half and leave medium and small mushrooms whole.

In a small saucepan, melt butter; add garlic, salt, pepper, and parsley flakes. About 30 minutes before grilling, pour butter mixture over mushrooms and toss. Lay on hot grill and grill until tender.

CLASSIC BREAD STUFFING

Serves 6

This stuffing is sure to become a regular addition to your Thanksgiving feast.

12 slices sandwich bread, toasted

¼ cup butter

½ medium onion, diced

1 cup chopped carrots

2 stalks celery, diced

2 cups chicken stock

1 teaspoon salt

½ teaspoon pepper

½ teaspoon poultry seasoning

3 eggs

1 cup milk

Tear toasted bread into pieces and place in a 9 x 13-inch baking dish.

In a saucepan, melt butter and sauté onion until translucent. Add carrots, celery, chicken stock, and seasonings; simmer until carrots are tender. Remove from heat.

In a small bowl, beat eggs and milk. Slowly pour egg mixture into broth mixture, stirring quickly so the eggs don't cook and make clumps. Pour mixture over bread pieces. Bake at 350°F for 35 minutes.

CREAMED LIMA BEANS (OR PEAS)

Serves 4

Add these to a meal of grilled pork chops and roasted sweet potatoes and you will be happy.

1 pint (about 2 cups) frozen lima beans, thawed

2 tablespoons water

1 tablespoon butter

1 teaspoon sugar

½ teaspoon salt

½ cup half-and-half

2 teaspoons cornstarch

In a saucepan, stir together lima beans, water, butter, sugar, and salt. Cover and simmer until tender but not soft (about 8 minutes). In a 1-cup liquid measuring cup, whisk together half-and-half and cornstarch. While stirring beans, add cream mixture, and keep stirring until thickened. Remove from heat. If the creamed lima beans are too thick, pour in a little more half-and-half and stir.

TIP: This is the same creaming method I use for peas. If buying peas, make sure they are labeled baby or petite peas. Cook peas 2 minutes before adding thickening. If they are too thick, pour in a little additional half-and-half and stir. Don't overcook peas or they will get chalky.

Pole lima beans

I grew up eating creamed lima beans (see p. 121). When I was younger I didn't appreciate them the way I do now. I didn't realize how much work lima beans are to start, plant, grow, pick, and shell. I also have learned to love the texture and flavor. They are delightful paired with grilled meat, sweet potatoes, and a salad. We also eat succotash, which is a mix of lima beans and corn, every Thanksgiving.

Each year, Mom saves the biggest pods of limas for seeds for the next year. In early spring she starts them in potting soil and then plants them in the garden when it's past the frost date. Unlike bush lima beans, pole limas climb up a trellis. Each plant has to be trained to climb up a string. Mom lets two runners climb the string and pinches back the remaining new runners so the energy can be put into the lima bean pod and not the stalk.

Mom usually plants around seventy-five plants each year, which yield around seventy to eighty pints of lima beans. Picking and shelling limas requires lots of time, but the reward is great.

We usually sit on Mom's porch to shell limas and watch the world go by. All through my growing-up years, my grandma Rhodes would come help us shell washtubs full of limas. She was an avid gardener all her life and was always willing to help Mom in the busy preserving months of summer.

When you preserve produce with family—that's my sister Faith with my daughter Natalie in the photo—it's more like play than work. Before you know it, those two tubs of limas are shelled and Mom is putting on pots of water to blanch the limas before they are put in the freezer.

I am still working on my lima bean growing skills, and I do depend on Mom's seventy-five plants each year. Dad keeps mentioning that the garden somehow stays the same size even though we girls have gotten married and there's only Dad and Mom at home. It's true: Mom keeps planting as much as she did when we lived at home because she keeps sharing her abundance with her girls each year.

ROASTED BROCCOLI

Serves 4

A flavorful and easy way to fix fresh broccoli. Don't worry if there are dark brown tips after roasting—they are full of flavor.

---

6 cups fresh broccoli spears

2 tablespoons olive oil

1 garlic clove, crushed

salt and pepper

Line a baking sheet with parchment paper. In a bowl, toss broccoli, oil, and garlic. Place evenly on the baking sheet and sprinkle with salt and pepper. Bake at 475°F for 15 minutes.

PERFECT BROCCOLI

Serves 4

Something about adding the sugar to the water makes this cooked broccoli method hard to beat.

½ cup water

1 teaspoon sugar

4 cups frozen or fresh chopped broccoli

salt

Combine water and sugar in a saucepan. Bring to a boil; add broccoli. Cover and cook 5–8 minutes, or until just tender. Sprinkle with salt and serve immediately.

STUFFED PEPPERS

Serves 12

I plant bell peppers in my garden each year just so I can make this recipe. I grew up eating stuffed peppers all summer long. In the summer we would eat fresh tomato sandwiches, corn on the cob, and stuffed peppers for supper.

4–6 large bell peppers

1 cup crushed crackers

2 cups shredded cheddar cheese

1 cup mayonnaise

2 teaspoons white vinegar

2 teaspoons sugar

¼ teaspoon seasoned salt

¼ teaspoon pepper

Seed and halve bell peppers. In a medium-sized bowl, mix together remaining ingredients. Fill bell pepper halves with mixture. If making ahead of time, wait to add crackers so that the filling won't be soggy.

RICE AND BEANS

Serves 4

I use this as a side to many of my main dishes. I like to use basmati rice for this and other recipes.

1 tablespoon oil

1½ cup uncooked rice, rinsed

1 teaspoon salt

1 tablespoon cream of coconut (optional)

1 (15½-ounce) can black beans, drained

2 cups water

Heat oil in a pot; add rice, salt, and cream of coconut, if desired. Sauté until rice starts to look slightly toasted (this adds flavor). Add black beans and water. Stir well. Cover and bring to a hard boil; turn to lowest heat and cook, covered, for 20 minutes. Remove from heat and let stand for 10 minutes. Fluff with a fork and serve.

TIP: Cream of coconut can usually be found in the mixed drink section of the grocery store.

BEEF AND PORK

We usually have a freezer full of locally raised beef and pork. For beef, we have found that purchasing a whole cow from a farm and then having it processed at a local butcher costs less than buying beef at the grocery store. Not only is it more economical; it tastes better too! For pork, we butcher a pig every year with my family. We vacuum-pack all the meat, and it stays fresh for a long time.

Buying in bulk and butchering may not work for everyone, because you need to have freezer space available, but these methods have worked well for us.

Classic Meat Loaf with Caramelized Topping

Beef Stroganoff

Taco Salad

Spaghetti with Flavorful Meat Sauce

Easy Lasagna

Stromboli

Friday Night Pizza

Steak and Cheese Subs

Barbecued Meatballs

Savory Meatballs

Poor Man's Steak

Cheesy Beef Enchiladas

Traditional Roast Beef

Sliced Beef with Creamy Horseradish Sauce

Roasted Pork Loin

Pulled Pork Barbecue

Grilled Pork Chops

Country Fried Pork Chops

Pork Chops with Mustard Sauce

Maple-Glazed Pork Chops

Pork Tacos with Pineapple Salsa

Oven Barbecued Ribs

CLASSIC MEAT LOAF
with Caramelized Topping
Serves 4–6

My go-to ground beef recipe when I need a quick meat dish. The caramelized topping finishes off this meat loaf perfectly.

1 tablespoon butter

1 onion, chopped

½ cup ketchup

1 egg, beaten

1 tablespoon white vinegar

1 tablespoon cornmeal

1 tablespoon brown sugar

1 teaspoon salt

½ teaspoon pepper

1 cup cracker crumbs

1 pound ground beef

Topping

⅓ cup ketchup

1 tablespoon brown sugar

2 teaspoons yellow mustard

several drops liquid smoke

In a small skillet, melt butter and sauté onion until starting to brown. Set aside to cool.

In a medium bowl, mix together ketchup, egg, vinegar, cornmeal, brown sugar, salt, and pepper. Stir well. Fold in sautéed onions, cracker crumbs, and ground beef, and mix just until combined. Overmixing can cause a tough and dense meat loaf. Line a baking sheet with parchment paper and form into a 4 x 9-inch loaf. Bake at 350°F for 35 minutes, or until internal temperature reaches 160°F.

Make topping: Stir together ingredients in a small bowl. Spread over top of cooked meat loaf. Broil at 400°F for 10 minutes more, or just until top caramelizes. Let stand 10 minutes before cutting so that meat loaf stays together.

BEEF STROGANOFF

Serves 4

I grew up eating stroganoff made with ground beef. This is a quick meal that your family will love, especially if you serve it with honey green beans and lettuce salad.

1 pound ground beef

½ onion, chopped

3 garlic cloves, crushed or minced

8 ounces fresh mushrooms, sliced, or 2 (4-ounce) cans sliced mushrooms, drained

2 cups milk

3 tablespoons unbleached white flour

1¼ teaspoon salt

½ teaspoon pepper

¼ teaspoon paprika

½ cup sour cream

12 ounces uncooked egg noodles

½ teaspoon salt

In a large skillet, brown ground beef with onion. Add garlic and mushrooms. Cook until mushrooms are tender.

In a bowl, whisk together milk, flour, 1¼ teaspoon salt, pepper, and paprika. Add to skillet and simmer until thickened. Stir in sour cream and simmer until heated through.

Cook egg noodles with ½ teaspoon salt according to package directions. Drain.

Serve stroganoff on a bed of egg noodles. Garnish with parsley, if desired.

TACO SALAD

Serves 6

If I call Joshua at work and ask him what to make for supper, he almost always requests taco salad.

1 pound ground beef

½ onion, chopped

1 (15½-ounce) can black beans, drained

1 (6-ounce) can tomato paste

1 quart (4 cups) tomato juice

2 tablespoons Taco Seasoning (p. 302)

2 tablespoons brown sugar

¼ teaspoon salt

¼ teaspoon red pepper flakes

corn chips

Toppings

shredded cheese

chopped lettuce

chopped tomatoes

sliced black olives

chopped onions

In a pot, brown ground beef with onions. Add remaining ingredients except for corn chips, and simmer for 30 minutes.

Serve on a bed of crushed corn chips with toppings. Drizzle with Ranch Dressing (p. 92).

SPAGHETTI
with Flavorful Meat Sauce
Serves 6–8

I like to mix ground beef and pork for my spaghetti sauce. Adding the cream at the end creates a lovely mellow tomato flavor that keeps you coming back for more. This is a large recipe; sometimes I freeze half the meat sauce and only cook half the spaghetti. Serve with Perfect Broccoli (p. 125) and a salad.

1 pound spaghetti

1 pound ground beef

1 pound ground pork sausage

1 medium onion, diced

4 garlic cloves, crushed

1 (6-ounce) can tomato paste

2 quarts (8 cups) tomato juice

¼ cup white wine

2 teaspoons brown sugar

1 tablespoon dried basil

2 teaspoons dried parsley

1 teaspoon salt

¼ teaspoon black pepper

¼ teaspoon red pepper flakes

2 tablespoons cornstarch, dissolved in ¼ cup cold water

1 cup half-and-half

Cook spaghetti in salted water until al dente according to package directions. Drain.

In a pot, brown beef, sausage, and onion. Add garlic, tomato paste, tomato juice, wine, brown sugar, basil, parsley, salt, pepper, and red pepper flakes and simmer on low for 30 minutes. Add cornstarch mixture and cook until thickened. Stir in half-and-half; add al dente spaghetti and simmer on low 5 minutes more, or until spaghetti is done. Serve with freshly grated Parmesan cheese.

EASY LASAGNA

Serves 10

A timeless recipe from Mom that's easy to assemble. You don't even need to precook your lasagna noodles before assembling. Serve with broccoli and salad.

9–12 uncooked lasagna noodles

Sauce

1 pound ground beef

1 onion, diced

2 garlic cloves, crushed

1 (6-ounce) can tomato paste

1 quart (4 cups) tomato juice

1½ cup water

2 tablespoons brown sugar

1 teaspoon dried oregano

1 teaspoon dried basil

1¼ teaspoon salt

½ teaspoon pepper

Cheese

16 ounces cottage cheese or ricotta cheese

1 egg, beaten

1 teaspoon dried parsley flakes

½ cup freshly grated Parmesan cheese

2 cups shredded mozzarella cheese

Make sauce: In a pot, brown ground beef with onion. Add remaining ingredients. Simmer on low for 15 minutes. (It will seem runny, but the uncooked lasagna noodles will soak up the liquid.)

In another bowl, mix together cottage cheese, egg, and parsley flakes.

Place 3–4 noodles in an ungreased 9 x 13-inch baking dish, top with a third of the meat sauce (about 2½ cups), then half the cottage cheese mixture, then half the Parmesan cheese. Repeat layers one more time. Top with last noodle layer and with remaining meat sauce.

Bake, covered, at 325°F for 45 minutes. Remove cover and sprinkle with mozzarella cheese. Bake, uncovered, for 15 minutes. Garnish with fresh basil, if desired.

STROMBOLI

Serves 4–6

As kids, my sisters and I could always choose our birthday supper menu, and stromboli was always a favorite. Of course, we grew up eating the Mennonite version—with yellow mustard, ham, salami, sausage, and American and mozzarella cheese. You can easily substitute cheddar for the American cheese if you prefer. This recipe makes nice calzones as well.

Dough

1 cup warm water

1 tablespoon active dry yeast

1 tablespoon olive oil

1 tablespoon honey

2½ cups unbleached white flour

1 teaspoon salt

Traditional filling

6–8 slices hard salami

1 pound ground pork sausage, browned

10 fresh mushrooms, sliced

½ onion, thinly sliced

1 (4-ounce) can black olives

1 jalapeño pepper, thinly sliced

2 cups shredded mozzarella cheese

½ cup freshly grated Parmesan cheese

freshly ground pepper, as desired

Mennonite filling

3 tablespoons yellow mustard

½ pound sliced ham

6 slices salami

¾ pound ground sausage, browned

6 slices American cheese

2 cups shredded mozzarella cheese

freshly ground pepper, as desired

Additional ingredients

1 egg, beaten

1 tablespoon water

dried oregano

marinara sauce, for dipping

Make dough: In a 2-cup liquid measuring cup, whisk together warm water, yeast, oil, and honey. In a medium bowl, combine flour and salt. Make a well in the middle of flour and pour in yeast mixture. Mix together with a fork until combined. Knead lightly and form into a smooth ball. Cover and let rise 20 minutes.

Sprinkle flour on counter. Knead the dough a little and sprinkle the top with flour. Roll out into a 12 x 20-inch rectangle. Layer either traditional filling or Mennonite filling ingredients down the center, in order listed. Sprinkle with pepper. Fold one side of dough over the filling and then wet the top edges with water. Fold the other side over top and seal ends, pinching tight. Carefully transfer to a greased baking sheet.

Make an egg wash: Mix together egg and water. Brush top of stromboli with egg wash and sprinkle with dried oregano. Bake at 400°F for 20 minutes. Cover with foil for a few minutes after removing from the oven to soften the crust. Slice and serve with marinara sauce.

You can make stromboli ahead of time and freeze before baking. Thaw completely and let rise before baking—around 2 hours.

TIP: To make calzones, divide dough recipe into 4 sections. Roll out into circles and top half the circle with pizza sauce and toppings. Brush edges with eggs wash, fold in half, and pinch edges shut. Place on greased baking sheet. Brush tops with egg wash and bake at 400°F for 15 minutes.

FRIDAY NIGHT PIZZA

Serves 4

Joshua loves pizza. He asks if we can eat it every Friday night. This dough is the same as the dough for Cheesy Breadsticks (p. 46) but is refrigerated for 2–3 days to create a chewy texture. See recipe tip below.

Dough

1 cup warm water

1 tablespoon active dry yeast

1 tablespoon olive oil

1 tablespoon honey

2½ cups unbleached white flour

1 teaspoon salt

Toppings

1 cup pizza sauce

2 cups shredded mozzarella cheese

1 cup fried sausage

5 slices bacon, fried and chopped

½ green or red bell pepper, sliced

1 small onion, sliced in rings

1 (2¼-ounce) can sliced black olives

fresh basil, chopped

freshly ground black pepper, as desired

Parmesan cheese, grated

In a 2-cup liquid measuring cup, whisk together warm water, yeast, oil, and honey. In a medium bowl, combine flour and salt. Make a well in the middle of flour and pour in yeast mixture. Mix together with a fork until combined. Knead lightly by hand and form into a smooth ball. Place in a greased bowl, cover; let it rise for at least 1–2 hours.

Line a baking sheet with parchment paper and grease lightly with oil. Oil your hands and spread out dough 1 inch away from the sides of the baking sheet. (It also works great using a 14-inch round pizza pan; oil well and dust with cornmeal.) Spread with toppings in order listed. Bake at 475°F for 10–12 minutes.

TIP: For a chewier pizza crust, refrigerate dough in an airtight container for 2–3 days. Remove from the refrigerator and let rise 2 hours before baking.

STEAK AND CHEESE SUBS

Serves 6

A flavor-filled man sandwich that's fun to make and eat.

Vegetables

2 tablespoons butter

1 green bell pepper, sliced

½ onion, sliced

salt and pepper

Meat

2 tablespoons butter

2 pounds sirloin steak, cut into
   ½-inch strips

1 tablespoon Worcestershire sauce

Montreal steak seasoning

salt and pepper

Sandwiches

6 hoagie rolls

butter, for spreading

mayonnaise, for spreading

12 slices Muenster cheese

Prepare vegetables: In a skillet, melt butter. Add bell pepper and onion and sprinkle with salt and pepper. Sauté until tender. Remove from skillet.

Prepare steak: In the same skillet, melt 2 tablespoons additional butter and add steak and Worcestershire sauce. Sprinkle with steak seasoning and salt and pepper as desired. Cook on high, stirring often. Once the steak starts to brown slightly, return the sautéed vegetables to the skillet and cook a few minutes more. Do not overcook. You want the steak to be pink in the middle, as this makes a juicy sandwich.

Assemble sandwiches: Cut open hoagie rolls and lay on baking sheet. Spread lightly with butter. Broil in oven until toasted. Remove from oven and spread mayonnaise on the bottom of each hoagie roll, then add the steak mixture. Top with cheese. Return to oven and broil until cheese is melted. Serve immediately. Use the leftover pan juices for a dipping sauce.

BARBECUED MEATBALLS

Serves 14

A classic meatball recipe topped with a flavorful sauce. I love this large recipe, which makes about 30 meatballs, because I can put one pan in the freezer to pull out on a busy day.

Meatballs

½ cup diced onion

1 cup milk

2 eggs

2 garlic cloves, crushed,
    or ½ teaspoon garlic powder

2 teaspoons chili powder

2 teaspoons salt

½ teaspoon pepper

3 pounds ground beef

1 cup rolled oats

1 cup cracker crumbs

Barbecue sauce

2 cups ketchup

⅔ cup brown sugar

1 garlic clove, crushed,
    or ½ teaspoon garlic powder

½ teaspoon liquid smoke

2 teaspoons lemon juice

pinch cayenne pepper

In a small skillet, sauté onion in a little oil until translucent. Set aside.

Make meatballs: In a large bowl, mix together milk, eggs, garlic, chili powder, salt, and pepper. Fold in ground beef, rolled oats, cracker crumbs, and onion. Mix just until combined. Form into meatballs using ¼ cup mixture per meatball. Place in a baking dish.

Make sauce: In a small bowl, mix together sauce ingredients. Top each meatball with a spoonful of sauce.

Bake at 350°F for 45 minutes, or until internal temperature reaches 160°F. Garnish with parsley flakes, if desired, and serve.

SAVORY MEATBALLS

Serves 14

I created this recipe, which also makes 30 meatballs, to have another version of meatballs. This creamy sauce is full of flavor—I love the combination of the cream, cheddar, and Dijon mustard.

Meatballs

1 cup milk

2 eggs

2 garlic cloves, crushed, or ½ teaspoon garlic powder

2 teaspoons chili powder

2 teaspoons salt

½ teaspoon pepper

3 pounds ground beef

1 cup rolled oats

1 cup cracker crumbs

½ cup diced onion

Sauce

2 cups half-and-half

4 ounces cream cheese, cubed

1 tablespoon Dijon mustard

2 cups shredded sharp cheddar

1 teaspoon salt

½ teaspoon pepper

¼ teaspoon garlic powder

Make meatballs: In a large bowl, mix together milk, eggs, garlic, chili powder, salt, and pepper. Fold in ground beef, rolled oats, cracker crumbs, and onion. Mix just until combined. Form into meatballs using ¼ cup mixture per meatball. Place in a baking dish.

Make sauce: In a small saucepan, bring half-and-half to a simmer. Add cream cheese and whisk until smooth. Add mustard, cheddar cheese, salt, pepper, and garlic powder. Stir until cheese is melted. Spoon on top of meatballs.

Bake at 350°F for 45 minutes, or until internal temperature reaches 160°F. Garnish with parsley flakes, if desired, and serve.

POOR MAN'S STEAK

Serves 4

This is one dish I learned to make for Joshua after we were married. He grew up eating poor man's steak, but I didn't. This creamy mushroom gravy pairs wonderfully with ground beef. Serve with mashed potatoes, because the extra gravy needs a home.

1 egg

¼ teaspoon Worcestershire sauce

1 dash liquid smoke

½ teaspoon salt

¼ teaspoon pepper

½ cup cracker crumbs

¼ cup minced onion

1 pound ground beef

2 tablespoons butter

8 ounces fresh mushrooms, sliced thick, or 2 (4-ounce) cans sliced mushrooms, drained

2 garlic cloves, crushed

Gravy

2 cups milk

2 tablespoons unbleached white flour

½ teaspoon salt

freshly ground pepper, to taste

¼ cup sour cream

In a medium bowl, mix together egg, Worcestershire sauce, liquid smoke, salt, pepper, cracker crumbs, and onion. Fold in ground beef and mix until just combined. Form into 7 round patties using ⅓ cup mixture per patty.

In a large skillet, melt butter, and add patties to skillet. Cook on medium heat until both sides are brown. Remove patties from the skillet.

Add mushrooms and garlic to pan drippings. Fry until garlic is soft and mushrooms are tender.

Make gravy: In a liquid measuring pitcher, whisk together milk, flour, salt, and pepper. While stirring, add milk mixture to skillet. Simmer until thickened. Add sour cream and stir until smooth. Return patties to skillet and simmer on low for 5 minutes.

CHEESY BEEF ENCHILADAS

Serves 4–6

We love these beef enchiladas. Who doesn't love cheese sauce? Serve with toppings of your choice. I use sour cream, chopped tomatoes, and chopped lettuce. Add Rice and Beans (p. 126) as a side and you have a full meal.

1 pound ground beef

1 onion, chopped

1 tablespoon Taco Seasoning (p. 302)

12 (8-inch) flour tortillas

Cheese sauce

½ cup butter

2 tablespoons unbleached white flour

2 cups milk

1 cup shredded Monterey Jack or cheddar cheese

¼ teaspoon salt

freshly ground black pepper, as desired

In a skillet, brown ground beef with onions. Add taco seasoning and stir well.

Fill each tortilla with ¼ cup of meat and roll up. Place in a greased 9 x 13-inch baking dish seam side down.

Make sauce: In a saucepan, melt butter and add flour, stirring until smooth. Cook for 1 minute. Add milk, cheese, salt, and pepper. Simmer on very low until thickened. Do not boil. Pour over tortillas and bake, covered, at 350°F for 25 minutes, or until bubbly.

TRADITIONAL ROAST BEEF

Serves 6

A Sunday lunch favorite. I use chicken stock instead of water because it makes a strong, flavorful broth. You can use this broth to cook noodles or to make a delicious gravy. Sometimes I fold chunks of beef into my noodles after they are cooked.

---

1 (3-pound) chuck roast

salt and pepper

olive oil

1 tablespoon brown sugar

⅓ cup white or red wine

1 bay leaf

4 cups chicken stock

Grab a nice chuck roast and season all sides with salt and pepper. Add a little oil to a skillet and sear all sides until medium brown (this adds lots of flavor). Place in a slow cooker. Add brown sugar, wine, and bay leaf, then pour chicken stock over all. Cook on low for 8 hours. Remove roast from broth and plate it. Strain broth, dip off fat, and use for gravy or cooking noodles.

NOTE: If serving this for Sunday lunch, cook this in the crockpot the night before. Leave the crockpot on warm while you are at church.

SLICED BEEF
with Creamy Horseradish Sauce
Serves 10–12

An elegant meat for special occasions. The horseradish sauce is so delightful paired with the sliced beef.

1 (5- to 6-pound) sirloin tip roast

oil

Rub

3 large garlic cloves, crushed

3 tablespoons brown sugar

1 tablespoon salt

1 tablespoon pepper

Creamy horseradish sauce

½ cup sour cream

½ cup mayonnaise

⅛ cup Dijon mustard

1 tablespoon cream-style horseradish

½ teaspoon lemon juice

½ teaspoon granulated sugar

¼ teaspoon salt

In a small bowl, mix together rub ingredients and rub on roast. Refrigerate for 3 hours.

In a large skillet, heat some oil and sear roast on all sides until medium brown.

Place roast in a roasting pan and roast, uncovered, at 300°F until center reaches 145°F (around 2–3 hours). Remove from oven and cover with foil. Let rest 30 minutes. Stir together sauce ingredients. Thinly slice roast just before serving and serve with creamy horseradish sauce.

ROASTED PORK LOIN

Serves 6

I think the trick to a good pork loin is roasting it slow and not overcooking it. A meat thermometer is a must when roasting pork.

1 (3- to 4-pound) boneless pork loin

Rub
3 tablespoons brown sugar
1 tablespoon salt
1 tablespoon pepper

In a small bowl, mix together rub ingredients and rub all over pork loin. Let stand 2 hours before roasting.

Place pork loin in a roasting pan and roast, uncovered, at 300°F until center reaches 145°F (about 1½ hour).

Remove from oven and cover. Let rest 20 minutes (do not skip this step!) and then slice thin before serving. Serve with barbecue sauce on the side.

PULLED PORK BARBECUE

Serves 6–8

This is an effortless way to make pulled pork. This works with most pork roast cuts, but I prefer a Boston butt. If you are in a hurry, skip the homemade barbecue sauce and use store-bought sauce. You can also cook any cut of pork roast this way and make a gravy with the broth.

1 (3- to 4-pound) pork Boston butt

olive oil

Rub

3 tablespoons brown sugar

1 tablespoon salt

1 tablespoon pepper

Barbecue sauce

1 tablespoon butter

½ cup sliced onion

¾ cup ketchup

⅓ cup white vinegar

½ cup water

1 tablespoon Worcestershire sauce

2 teaspoons lemon juice

¼ teaspoon liquid smoke

3 tablespoons brown sugar

2 teaspoons dry mustard

½ teaspoon salt

½ teaspoon pepper

In a small bowl, mix together rub ingredients and rub all over the pork. Heat a little olive oil in a pot and sear pork on all sides until brown. Place in a slow cooker and cook on low for 8 hours.

Make sauce: In a saucepan, melt butter and add onions. Sauté onions until translucent. Add remaining ingredients and simmer on low for 10 minutes.

After the pork is done, place it on a plate and pull it apart with two forks. Add pork to the barbecue sauce and simmer for a few minutes. Serve on a pretzel bun with coleslaw.

GRILLED PORK CHOPS

Serves 4–6

An elegant meat for guests that is easy to prepare.

---

8 pork chops
¼ cup butter, melted

Rub

3 tablespoons brown sugar

1 tablespoon salt

1 tablespoon pepper

In a small bowl, mix together rub ingredients and sprinkle all over pork chops. Refrigerate 2–4 hours before grilling.

Place pork chops on a hot grill and brush each side with butter while grilling. Grill until insides are no longer pink, or until internal temperature just reaches 145°F. Do not overcook. Serve with barbecue sauce on the side.

COUNTRY FRIED PORK CHOPS

Serves 4–6

This recipe is Southern comfort food. Serve with fluffy mashed potatoes and your dining companions will even wash the dishes.

---

8 boneless pork chops

1 cup unbleached white flour

3 tablespoons butter

seasoned salt

salt and pepper

Gravy

1 cup half-and-half

1 cup milk

2 tablespoons unbleached white flour

Dredge pork chops in 1 cup flour. Melt butter in skillet and add pork chops. Sprinkle the first side with seasoned salt and the other side with salt and pepper. Fry until done, or until center reaches 145°F. Remove from skillet.

Whisk together half-and-half, milk, and 2 tablespoons flour. Add to pan drippings. Simmer until thickened. Taste gravy and add more salt and pepper if desired. Return the pork chops to the skillet with the gravy and simmer on low for a few minutes.

Butchering day

I vividly remember butchering day as a child. One day Mom asked if I would rather go to school or come with them to butchering day. I told her I'd rather come to the "pig meet'n." I'm not sure what the pigs were meeting other than their end, but for years after that, our family called butchering day the "pig meet'n."

Since we've been married, Joshua and I butcher a pig every January with my family. Joshua has really enjoyed learning how to process a pig and also enjoys the fresh pork in the freezer.

It's amazing how much meat you can process from a whole pig. Dad starts by cutting out the prime cuts of meat, like roasts and loins, to leave whole. Then we cut up the remaining meat and separate the fat from the red meat. The red meat is ground into sausage, and the fat is cooked down to make lard.

We trim the meat off the bones as best we can, then we throw them in a cast iron kettle of boiling water. Then we cook them for meat pudding and broth, which is later made into *pon haus*. *Pon haus* is a mixture of broth, meat, and cornmeal that is sliced and fried.

Here's how we make it: Once the bones have simmered for several hours, we remove them from the kettle and pick off the meat. We then run the cooked meat through a sausage grinder to make it fine. The broth from the bones is strained and set aside. We brown the cooked meat in the kettle and remove some "meat pudding," as we call it, for Grandma (she enjoys it more than we do). As a child I remember eating the meat pudding on cooked hominy with apple butter.

Then we add the broth back to the kettle along with cornmeal, salt, and pepper. We take turns stirring the mixture for fifteen minutes. When it starts to stiffen, we pour it into loaf pans. Once it has set, we slice and fry it in a hot griddle until crisp. There you have it: *pon haus*, a family favorite. People like eating it different ways. I like to drizzle mine with maple syrup, but Joshua prefers his with Dijon mustard.

The rest of the year I enjoy pulling pork out of our freezer. We have *pon haus* or sausage to enjoy for breakfast. I also like to mix sausage and ground beef in my recipes. In the summer there are pork chops for grilling and pork roasts to slow-cook for Pulled Pork Barbecue (p. 161).

There is something satisfying about knowing where your meat comes from. If you process your meat or vegetables yourself, you are a bit more responsible with it. You make sure it doesn't go to waste, because you know how much work it took, and that precious food just can't easily be replaced.

PORK CHOPS
with Mustard Sauce
Serves 4–6

This recipe offers an elegant way to dress up pork chops. The tangy mustard sauce is great paired with a side of baked sweet potatoes.

8 boneless pork chops
3 tablespoons butter

Rub
3 tablespoons brown sugar
1 tablespoon salt
1 tablespoon pepper

Sauce
1 tablespoon butter
1 garlic clove, crushed
3 tablespoons white wine
⅔ cup half-and-half
2 tablespoons Dijon mustard
2 teaspoons lemon juice

In a small bowl, mix together rub ingredients and rub on pork chops. Refrigerate 2 hours before frying.

In a skillet, melt 3 tablespoons butter and sear pork chops 2 minutes per side, or until center reaches 145°F. Place in a baking dish and place in a 200°F oven to keep warm while making the sauce.

In the skillet with the pan drippings, add 1 tablespoons butter and sauté garlic until fragrant. Add wine and deglaze the skillet. Add half-and-half and mustard. Simmer until sauce thickens. Remove from heat and add lemon juice. Drizzle over pork chops.

MAPLE-GLAZED PORK CHOPS

Serves 4–6

Maple syrup is one of my favorite flavors to pair with pork. The mushrooms add texture and an elegant touch.

8 boneless pork chops

3 tablespoons butter

8 ounces fresh mushrooms, sliced

½ cup chicken stock

⅓ cup maple syrup

Rub

3 tablespoons brown sugar

1 tablespoon salt

1 tablespoon pepper

In a small bowl, mix together rub ingredients and rub on pork chops. Refrigerate 2 hours before frying.

In a skillet, melt butter. Add pork chops and fry until done, 5–6 minutes total, or until internal temperature reaches 145°F. Size and thickness can make a difference. When done, remove from skillet.

Add mushrooms to pan drippings. Sauté until tender. Add chicken stock and maple syrup and cook on high until sauce reduces and thickens. Return pork chops to skillet and heat for 1 minute, or until heated through.

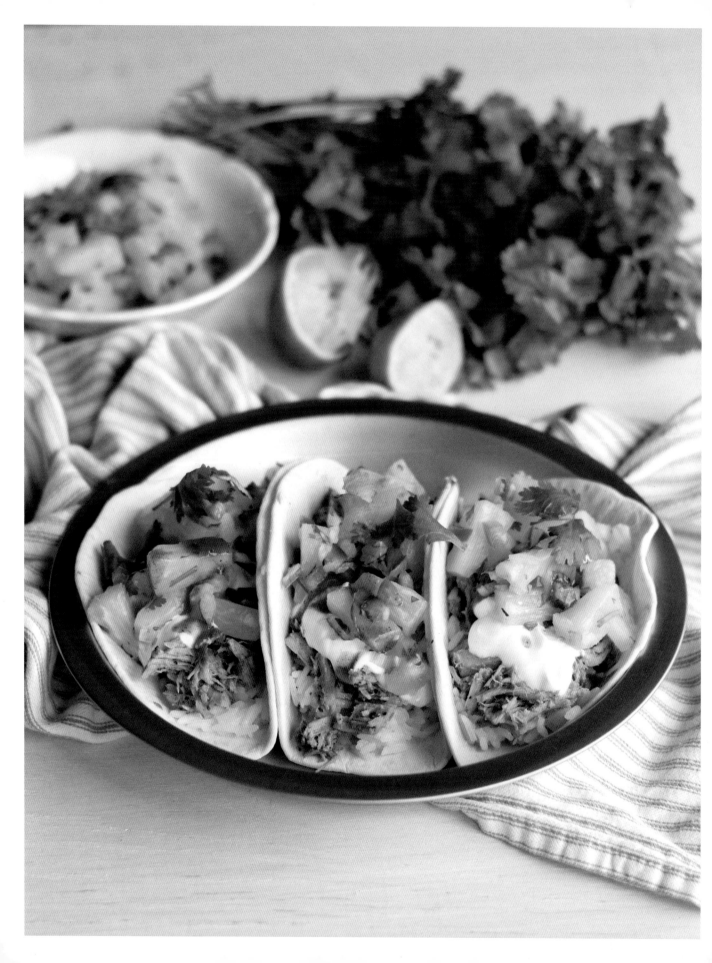

PORK TACOS
with Pineapple Salsa
Serves 8

Pork tacos are my favorite kind of taco. They are so delightful topped with pineapple salsa and sour cream.

2 cups uncooked basmati rice

1 (4- to 5-pound) boneless pork loin

24 (6-inch) flour or corn tortillas

1 (8-ounce) container sour cream

Rub

3 tablespoons brown sugar

1 tablespoon salt

1 tablespoon pepper

1 teaspoon paprika

1 teaspoon dried oregano

½ teaspoon red pepper flakes

Pineapple salsa

1 (20-ounce) can pineapple tidbits, drained well (fresh pineapple works too)

½ jalapeño pepper, minced

½ red onion, diced

¼ cup chopped fresh cilantro

juice of ½ lime

Cook rice according to package directions. In a small bowl, mix together rub ingredients and rub all over pork loin.

In a small bowl, mix together salsa ingredients. Refrigerate so flavors can blend.

Place pork loin in a roasting pan and roast, covered, at 250°F for 4 hours. Remove from oven and shred with tongs right in the roasting pan. The broth adds wonderful flavor.

Spoon into tortillas and serve with rice, pineapple salsa, and lots of sour cream.

OVEN BARBECUED RIBS

Serves 6

I've made this recipe for many of Joshua's birthday suppers. These ribs are stress free in terms of preparation and hard to beat in terms of taste.

---

1 large rack pork spare ribs (about 5 pounds)

Rub

3 tablespoons brown sugar

1 tablespoon salt

1 tablespoon pepper

Barbecue sauce

1 cup ketchup

2 tablespoons orange juice

¼ teaspoon liquid smoke

¼ cup brown sugar

1 teaspoon dry mustard

¼ teaspoon cayenne pepper

In a small bowl, mix together rub ingredients and rub on ribs. Refrigerate 2 hours before baking.

In a 2-cup liquid measuring cup, mix together sauce ingredients. Reserve ½ cup sauce and set aside.

Place ribs in a large roasting pan and add 1 inch of water. (If you don't have a large roasting pan, a baking sheet covered in foil will work.) Cover and roast at 300°F for 1 hour. Drain off liquid and top with remaining barbecue sauce.

Increase oven temperature to 350°F and bake, covered, 1 hour more. Remove cover and broil at 400°F for 10 minutes until top caramelizes. Cut ribs into serving-sized sections. Place on a large serving platter. Heat reserved sauce and drizzle over ribs before serving.

TIP: The ribs should pull apart easily with a fork but not fall off the bone. If they do not pull apart easily, they need to be roasted longer. Some ribs are thicker than others.

CHICKEN AND SEAFOOD

We really enjoy chicken. I have tried many brands of chicken and have found an antibiotic- and hormone-free brand that I like. I like boneless, skinless chicken thighs that come in a tray of eight; it's the perfect amount for our little family. I stock up every couple of weeks and just freeze the trays of chicken. They are handy to pull out in the morning and place in the sink to thaw for supper that evening.

We don't eat lots of seafood, but we do enjoy it for special occasions. I do make sure I purchase wild-caught seafood. We grew up eating shrimp at Christmas, so it has special memories for me.

Creamy Italian Chicken and Pasta

Chicken Parmesan

Chicken Marsala

Spring Roll Rice Bowls
with Sweet Garlic and Lime Dressing

Fiesta Burrito Bowls

Honey Barbecue Boneless Wings

Chicken Potpie

Chicken Fajitas

Mango Chicken Curry

Cajun Chicken with Avocado

Grilled Spicy Peach-Glazed Chicken

Grilled Honey Mustard Chicken

Grilled Maple Barbecued Chicken

Citrus Grilled Chicken

Classic Grilled Chicken

Grilled Chicken Pitas

Cornmeal-Crusted Chicken Tenders

Crispy Chicken Nuggets

Honey Roasted Chicken

Herb Roasted Chicken Thighs and Potatoes

Whole Roasted Chicken

Teriyaki Chicken and Fried Rice

Citrus Shrimp Kabobs

Shrimp Alfredo

Classic Steamed Shrimp with Cocktail Sauce

Baked Fish

Low Country Boil

Crab Cakes

CREAMY ITALIAN CHICKEN AND PASTA

Serves 4–6

I love to pan-sear meats and make a savory pan sauce with the flavorful drippings. This one is packed with flavor and is pleasing to the eye as well.

Pasta

¾ pound (3 cups) uncooked penne pasta

1 teaspoon salt

1 tablespoon olive oil

Chicken

3 large chicken breasts

salt and pepper

3 tablespoons butter

3 large garlic cloves, crushed

12 grape tomatoes, halved

⅓ cup white wine

1 cup half-and-half

1 cup milk

1 tablespoon cornstarch

1 teaspoon dried parsley flakes

½ teaspoon salt

¼ cup freshly grated Parmesan cheese

Cook pasta with 1 teaspoon salt according to package directions. Strain and coat with olive oil. This helps keep it from sticking together.

With a sharp knife, slice chicken breasts in half lengthwise. Sprinkle both sides with salt and pepper.

In a skillet, melt butter and add chicken. Spread a little crushed garlic on top of each piece of chicken. Fry on medium heat, uncovered, until almost done. Flip and fry other side until golden brown. (Cook 3–4 minutes per side, or until center reaches 165°F.) Remove chicken from skillet.

Add tomatoes to pan drippings, sliced side down. Fry until browned. Remove from skillet and pour in wine. Simmer until it reduces to half. In a liquid measuring cup, whisk together half-and-half, milk, and cornstarch. Pour into wine reduction and simmer until slightly thickened. Add parsley flakes and salt.

Return chicken and tomatoes to the skillet and top with cheese. Cover and simmer for 5 minutes. Serve over pasta. Season to taste with salt.

TIP: A good method for cutting chicken is to place your non-cutting hand flat on top of the chicken breast and apply pressure. Then use your knife to cut down the middle of the breast.

CHICKEN PARMESAN

Serves 4–6

A classic Italian dish that children and adults will love.

3 large chicken breasts

1 cup buttermilk

¼ cup butter

1 pound uncooked spaghetti

1 teaspoon salt

1 tablespoon olive oil

Breading

1 cup panko bread crumbs

1 cup unbleached white flour

1 teaspoon dried parsley flakes

2 teaspoons salt

¼ teaspoon pepper

Sauce

½ cup white cooking wine

8 ounces fresh mushrooms, sliced

2 garlic cloves, crushed or minced

1 (28-ounce) can diced tomatoes

2 tablespoons tomato paste

1 teaspoon brown sugar

½ teaspoon dried basil

½ teaspoon dried parsley

¼ teaspoon salt

¼ teaspoon pepper

⅛ teaspoon red pepper flakes

1 cup shredded mozzarella cheese

¼ cup freshly grated Parmesan cheese

In a pie pan, mix together breading ingredients. With a sharp knife, slice chicken breasts in half. Dip chicken in buttermilk, then coat with breading.

In a large skillet, melt butter. Add chicken. Fry on medium heat, uncovered, until mostly done. Flip and fry other side until golden brown. Remove chicken from skillet and place in a 9 x 13-inch baking dish. (If frying in two sections, add more butter for the second skillet.)

Make sauce: Add wine to pan drippings and reduce to half (about 1 minute). Add mushrooms and garlic and sauté until tender. Add tomatoes, tomato paste, brown sugar, basil, parsley, salt, pepper, and red pepper flakes. Simmer for 10 minutes. Pour sauce over chicken and top with mozzarella cheese and Parmesan cheese. Bake at 350°F for 20 minutes.

Cook spaghetti with 1 teaspoon salt according to package directions. Strain and coat with olive oil. This helps keep it from sticking together.

Serve chicken over pasta and sprinkle with additional freshly grated Parmesan cheese and fresh parsley, if desired.

TIP: To avoid some of the mess of sticky fingers, try to keep one hand dry and one hand wet when breading chicken and other meats.

TIP: If I have time, I soak the chicken in the buttermilk in the refrigerator for 1–2 hours before coating with breading. Soaking in buttermilk ahead of time tenderizes the chicken through the actions of enzymes naturally present in buttermilk.

CHICKEN MARSALA

Serves 4–6

Another Italian classic showcasing mushrooms with a lighter pan sauce.

¾ pound (3 cups) uncooked penne pasta

1 teaspoon salt

1 tablespoon olive oil

3 large chicken breasts

salt and pepper

3 tablespoons butter

½ cup unbleached white flour

1 pound fresh mushrooms, sliced thick

2 large garlic cloves, minced

1 cup marsala wine

1 tablespoon cornstarch

1 cup chicken stock

2 tablespoons cold butter, cubed

1 teaspoon lemon juice

freshly grated Parmesan cheese

Cook pasta with 1 teaspoon salt according to package directions. Strain and coat with olive oil. This helps keep it from sticking together.

With a sharp knife, slice chicken breasts in half lengthwise. Sprinkle both sides with salt and pepper.

Melt butter in large skillet. Dredge chicken in flour and add to skillet. Fry on medium heat, uncovered, until mostly done. Flip and fry until done (3–4 minutes per side, or until center reaches 165°F). Remove from skillet and place in an oven-safe dish.

Add mushrooms and garlic to pan drippings and sprinkle with salt; add a little butter to pan if needed. Sauté until tender. Add wine and bring to a boil for a few seconds to cook out the alcohol. Dissolve cornstarch in chicken stock and add to pan. Simmer at a rolling boil for 5 minutes, or until the sauce thickens and reduces a bit.

When the sauce is close to done, turn on the oven to broil at 400°F and heat chicken for 3–5 minutes until sizzling hot. This crisps it up a bit but doesn't dry out the meat.

Once sauce is slightly thickened, remove from heat. Add cold butter cubes and whisk until melted. Stir in lemon juice. Season to taste with salt and pepper.

Place hot chicken on a bed of pasta. Pour mushroom sauce over and sprinkle with a little freshly grated Parmesan cheese.

SPRING ROLL RICE BOWLS
with Sweet Garlic and Lime Dressing
Serves 4

I recently started making rice bowls for my family. This one is full of vibrant flavors. Use the vegetables as a guide and be creative! All the textures and colors make these fun to eat.

2 cups uncooked basmati rice

8 chicken thighs

oil

Marinade

⅓ cup olive oil

1 tablespoon Dijon mustard

juice of 1 lemon

juice of 1 lime

2 large garlic cloves, crushed or
   minced

1 tablespoon granulated sugar

1 teaspoon parsley flakes

1 teaspoon salt

½ teaspoon pepper

Vegetables

4 cups sliced red and green cabbage

1 cucumber, sliced

1 red bell pepper, sliced

1 cup chopped tomatoes

½ cup chopped spring onions

1 cup shredded carrots

fresh cilantro

Sweet garlic and lime dressing

⅓ cup canola oil

⅓ cup lime juice

¼ cup soy sauce

2 tablespoons rice vinegar

¼ cup brown sugar

2 garlic cloves, crushed

Cook rice according to package directions.

In a 2-cup liquid measuring cup, mix together marinade. Place chicken thighs in a gallon-sized resealable plastic bag and pour in marinade. Seal bag and flip until all thighs are coated in marinade. Marinate in refrigerator for 2–4 hours. In a hot skillet coated with oil, fry the chicken thighs until done. Slice into thin strips while hot and return to your skillet to keep warm.

Prepare vegetables and set aside.

In a bowl, combine dressing ingredients and blend well with an immersible blender.

To assemble: Start with a bed of rice, then top with chicken and vegetables. Drizzle with dressing and sprinkle with cilantro.

FIESTA BURRITO BOWLS

Serves 4

A one-dish meal that's great for a last-minute supper.

1½ cup uncooked rice

1 teaspoon salt

6 chicken thighs

2 tablespoons olive oil

1 tablespoon Taco Seasoning (p. 302)

2 cups frozen corn, thawed

1 (15-ounce) can black beans, drained

salt and pepper

Cook rice with 1 teaspoon salt according to package directions.

Cut chicken into 2-inch pieces. In a skillet, fry chopped chicken thighs in oil and sprinkle with taco seasoning. When chicken is done, add corn and black beans. Sprinkle with salt and pepper as desired and simmer until beans are tender. Serve over rice and top with toppings of your choice. I usually use lettuce, tomato, and chopped onion, and drizzle with Ranch Dressing (p. 92).

HONEY BARBECUE BONELESS WINGS

Serves 4–6

I love a good boneless chicken wing. This one has a good mix of heat and sweet.

8 boneless, skinless chicken thighs

seasoned salt

unbleached white flour, for coating chicken

oil, for frying

Sauce

¼ cup hot sauce

¼ cup ketchup

¼ cup honey

1 tablespoon dark molasses

1 teaspoon lemon juice

¼ teaspoon black pepper

2 dashes garlic powder

2 dashes cayenne pepper

Mix together sauce ingredients and set aside.

Cut chicken thighs into 1½-inch pieces. Sprinkle with seasoned salt and then coat with flour.

In a deep skillet, add 2 inches of oil and heat on medium-high. Add chicken to skillet in batches and fry for 4–5 minutes, turning periodically, until golden brown. Place in a 9-inch baking dish and pour sauce over chicken. Stir to make sure chicken is coated evenly. Broil at 400°F for 10 minutes, stirring halfway.

TIP: To tell whether oil is hot enough, drop in a small piece of bread to see if it bubbles and comes back to the top. If so, the oil is ready.

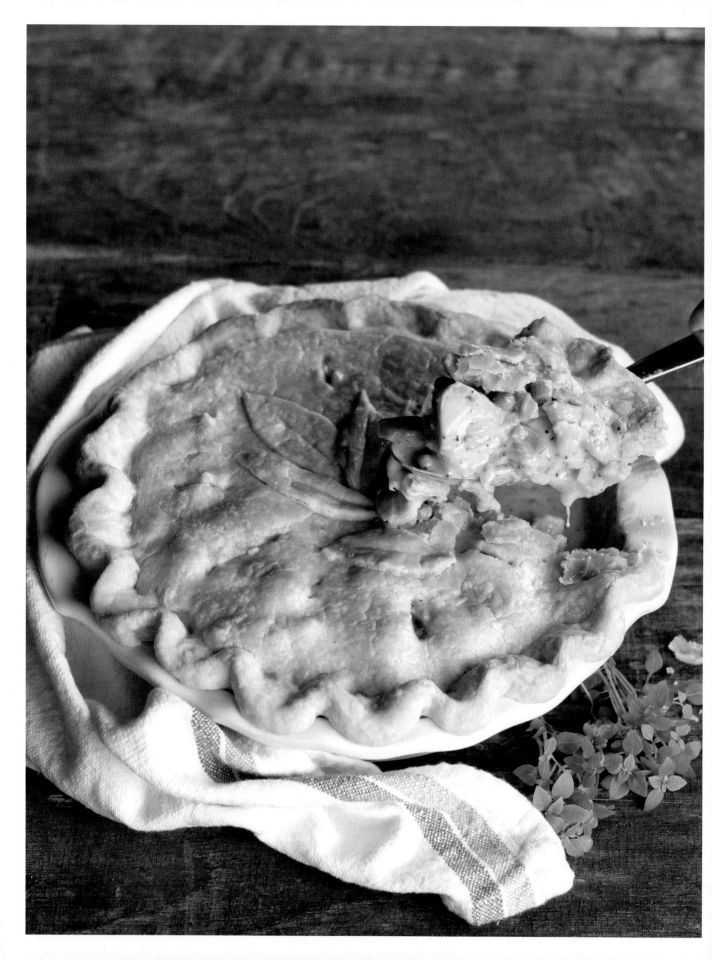

CHICKEN POTPIE

Serves 4–6

If you or anyone in your household wants to be comforted, make this recipe. Chicken potpie is a traditional old-fashioned dish with a flaky crust and filled with a creamy filling. If you want a quicker version of this, try Chicken and Dumpling Soup (p. 63).

---

1 double-crust pastry for a 10-inch pie (p. 251)

Chicken and vegetables

8 boneless, skinless chicken thighs

2 tablespoons butter

1 teaspoon seasoned salt

½ teaspoon pepper

1 cup chopped carrots

½ cup chopped celery

1 cup frozen peas, thawed

Sauce

3 tablespoons butter

1 medium onion, thinly sliced

⅓ cup unbleached white flour

½ teaspoon salt

½ teaspoon pepper

1¾ cup chicken stock

⅔ cup half-and-half

To brush on top of crust

1 egg, beaten

1 tablespoon water

Using a 10-inch pie pan, roll out half the pie pastry for the bottom pie crust and use the remaining dough for the top crust.

Cut chicken thighs into 1-inch pieces. In a large saucepan, melt 2 tablespoons butter, add chicken, and sprinkle with seasoned salt and pepper. Cook until no longer pink and starting to brown. Add carrots and celery. Cook until carrots are almost tender. Add peas and cook 1 minute more. Remove chicken and vegetables from saucepan.

Make sauce: In the same saucepan, melt 3 tablespoons additional butter and add onion. Cook until onion is translucent. Add flour, salt, and pepper and stir until smooth. Stirring continuously, pour in chicken stock and half-and-half. Simmer until thickened. Return chicken and vegetables to the pan and stir until combined.

Fill pie shell with filling. (You may have a little extra; just grab a spoon and comfort yourself.) Cover the top with the other rolled-out crust and seal the edges. Cut away excess dough and crimp edges. Make several small slits in the top so steam can escape. In a small bowl, whisk egg and water and then brush over top of crust.

Bake at 350°F for 45 minutes. Cool 10 minutes before serving so the filling can thicken a little.

CHICKEN FAJITAS

Serves 6

These chicken fajitas are packed with vibrant flavors and colors. Don't be scared to add the sliced jalapeño—it's not that hot once it's cooked. You could also skip the tortillas and make this recipe into fajita bowls. This chicken is also delicious when grilled. Just marinate the chicken thighs whole and slice into strips after grilling.

---

8 boneless, skinless chicken thighs

1 tablespoon butter

1 onion, sliced

1 green bell pepper, sliced

salt and pepper

6–10 (10-inch) flour tortillas

Marinade

1 jalapeño pepper, sliced

2 garlic cloves, minced or crushed

juice of 1 lime

¼ cup olive oil

1 teaspoon chili powder

1 teaspoon ground cumin

1 teaspoon black pepper

1 teaspoon salt

Toppings

Rice and Beans (p. 126)

Ranch Dressing (p. 92)

chopped tomatoes

guacamole

Slice chicken into ½-inch strips. In a medium bowl, mix together marinade ingredients. Add chicken and toss with marinade. Let stand for 30 minutes.

Melt butter in skillet. Add onions and bell peppers. Sprinkle with salt and pepper. Sauté until tender. Remove from skillet.

Add chicken with marinade to skillet, cover, and cook on medium heat until just done. Return bell peppers and onions to the skillet and simmer, uncovered, for a few minutes. (If it's still really juicy, cook on high until juices reduce.) Use tongs to place mixture in tortillas and top with toppings of your choice. The possibilities are endless!

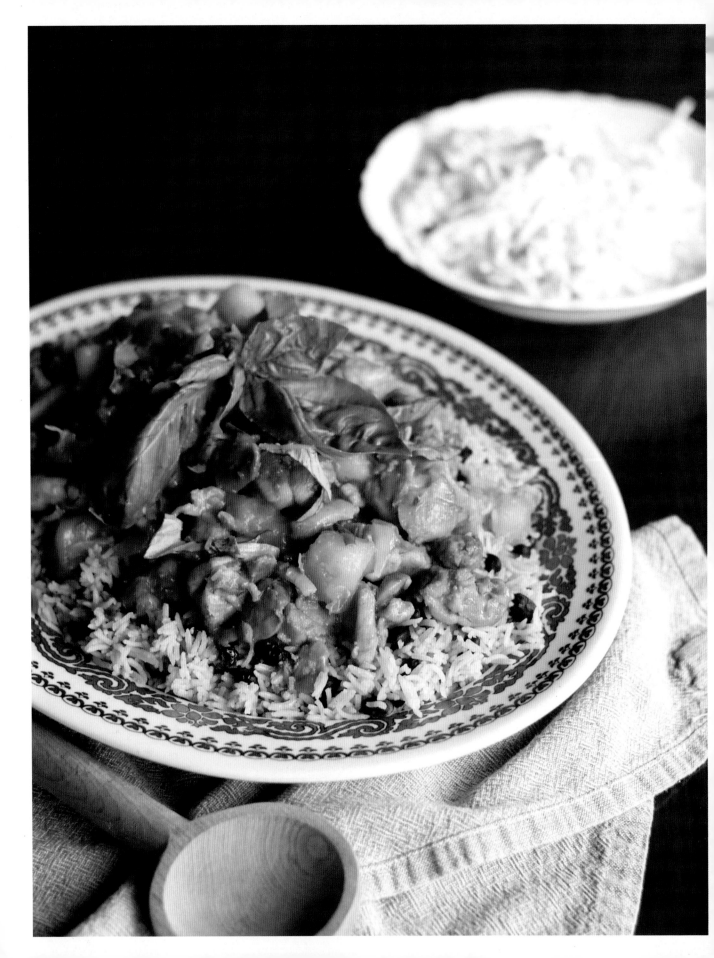

MANGO CHICKEN CURRY

Serves 6

I created this recipe in order to use up some ripe mangos, and it has been a favorite ever since. It's delightful served with Rice and Beans (p. 126) and thinly sliced cabbage tossed in Classic Creamy Dressing (p. 90).

8 chicken thighs

3 tablespoons olive oil

1 onion, thinly sliced

2 cups chopped fresh mango (may also use frozen)

1 tablespoon lemon juice

fresh basil, for garnish

Seasoning mixture

1 teaspoon salt

1 teaspoon turmeric

1 teaspoon white pepper

1 teaspoon cayenne pepper

Cut chicken into 2-inch pieces. Heat a large skillet and coat well with olive oil. In a small bowl, mix together seasoning mixture. Sprinkle evenly on chicken and stir with hands to make sure chicken is evenly coated. Add chicken to skillet and fry until golden brown.

Add the sliced onions; cover and simmer until onions are tender. Add mango; cover and simmer until mango is soft and juices start to release. Add lemon juice. (If the mixture seems too juicy, uncover and simmer until juices reduce a bit.)

Garnish with fresh basil.

CAJUN CHICKEN

with Avocado

Serves 4–6

Avocados have a way of brightening up any dish.

---

3 large chicken breasts

1 tablespoon Cajun seasoning

1 teaspoon salt

1 teaspoon pepper

canola oil, for frying

Topping

3 large avocados, cubed

¼ onion, diced

juice of ½ lemon

salt and pepper, to taste

In a small bowl, mix together topping ingredients and refrigerate so flavors can blend.

With a sharp knife, slice chicken breasts in half lengthwise.

Mix together Cajun seasoning, salt, and pepper. Sprinkle both sides of chicken with seasoning mixture and let stand a few minutes. Heat ⅛ inch of oil in a skillet and fry chicken on medium heat until nearly done. Flip and fry until done (3–4 minutes per side, or until center reaches 165°F).

Serve over Rice and Beans (p. 126) and top with avocado topping.

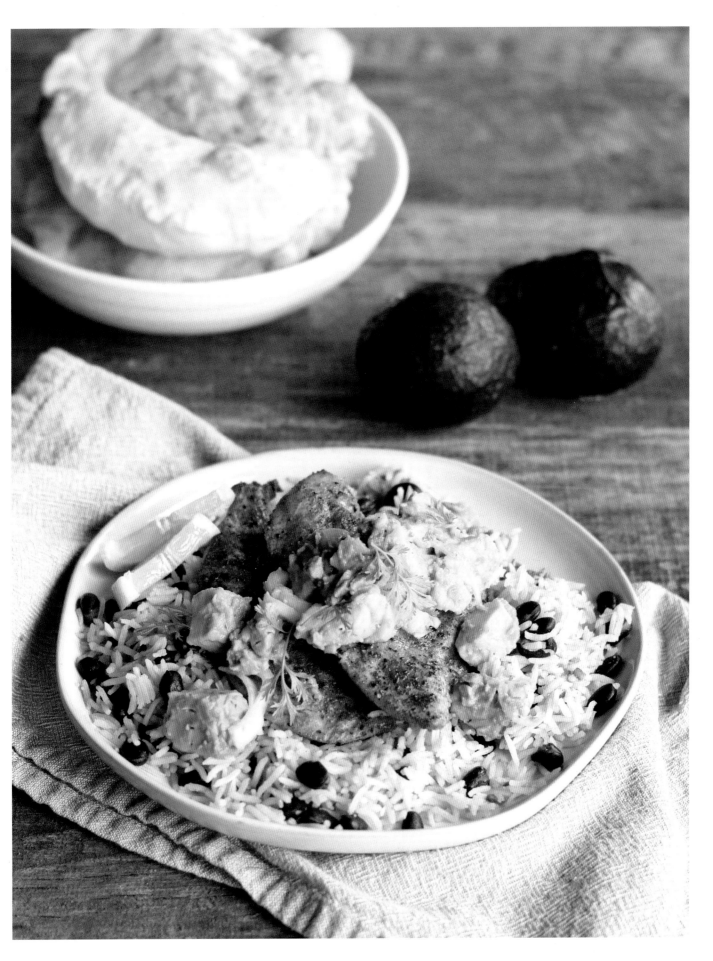

GRILLED SPICY PEACH-GLAZED CHICKEN

Serves 4–6

This dish is a mix of spice and sweet. Go ahead and eat three or so—chicken tenders are small.

2 pounds uncooked chicken tenders

Marinade

½ cup peach preserves

¼ cup oil

2 tablespoons barbecue sauce

1 tablespoon Dijon mustard

1 tablespoon white vinegar

1 large garlic clove, crushed

1 jalapeño pepper, diced

1 teaspoon salt

¼ teaspoon pepper

In a 2-cup liquid measuring cup, mix together marinade and reserve ¼ cup for glaze. In a gallon-sized resealable plastic bag, add chicken tenders and pour in remaining marinade. Seal bag and flip until chicken is fully coated in marinade. Marinate in refrigerator for 3–4 hours. Grill until done (around 4 minutes per side, or until center reaches 165°F).

Heat reserved marinade in small saucepan to use as a glaze, and drizzle over chicken before serving.

GRILLED HONEY MUSTARD CHICKEN

Serves 4–6

Everyone loves honey mustard. This chicken is also great sliced on top a summer garden salad.

8 boneless, skinless chicken thighs

Marinade

⅓ cup honey

3 tablespoons yellow mustard

2 tablespoons white vinegar

1 tablespoon Worcestershire sauce

1 teaspoon poultry seasoning

1 teaspoon salt

½ teaspoon pepper

⅛ teaspoon cayenne pepper

In a 2-cup liquid measuring cup, mix together marinade and reserve ¼ cup for drizzling at the end. In a gallon-sized resealable plastic bag, add chicken thighs and pour in remaining marinade. Seal bag and flip until all thighs are coated in marinade. Marinate in refrigerator for 3–4 hours. Grill until done (around 10 minutes per side, or until center reaches 165°F).

Heat reserved marinade and drizzle over chicken before serving.

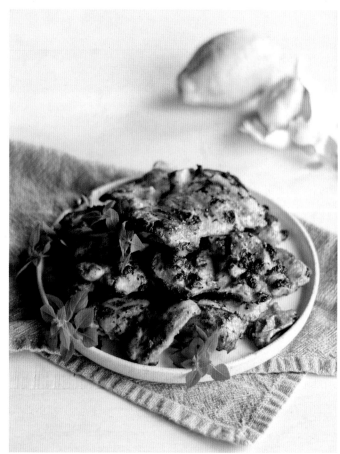

GRILLED MAPLE BARBECUED CHICKEN

Serves 4–6

A great barbecued chicken dish that is a tasty mix of sweet and smoky.

10 boneless, skinless chicken thighs

Marinade

⅓ cup maple syrup

⅓ cup barbecue sauce

3 tablespoons white vinegar

2 teaspoons Worcestershire sauce

½ teaspoon dry mustard

1 teaspoon salt

¼ teaspoon pepper

In a 2-cup liquid measuring cup, mix together marinade and reserve ¼ cup for drizzling at the end. In a gallon-sized resealable plastic bag, add chicken thighs and pour in remaining marinade. Seal bag and flip until all thighs are coated in marinade. Marinate in refrigerator for 3–4 hours. Grill until done (around 10 minutes per side, or until center reaches 165°F).

Heat reserved marinade and drizzle over chicken before serving.

CITRUS GRILLED CHICKEN

Serves 4–6

This is my favorite grilled chicken recipe. The flavors are so vibrant. It's very versatile and is delicious on top of salads or rice bowls. Be sure to try the Spring Roll Rice Bowl recipe (p. 183) using this marinade.

8 boneless, skinless chicken thighs

Marinade

⅓ cup olive oil

1 tablespoon Dijon mustard

juice of 1 lemon

juice of 1 lime

2 large garlic cloves, crushed or minced

1 tablespoon sugar

1 teaspoon parsley flakes

1 teaspoon salt

½ teaspoon pepper

In a 2-cup liquid measuring cup, mix together marinade. In a gallon-sized resealable plastic bag, add chicken thighs and pour in marinade. Seal bag and flip until all thighs are coated in marinade. Marinate in refrigerator for 2–4 hours. Grill until done (around 10 minutes per side, or until center reaches 165°F).

TIP: To get maximum juice from lemons and limes, microwave for 20–30 seconds before squeezing.

CLASSIC GRILLED CHICKEN

Serves 4–6

This is Joshua's favorite grilled chicken. It also works great with bone-in chicken thighs; just be sure to allow more time for grilling.

8–10 boneless, skinless chicken thighs

Marinade

½ cup water

½ cup white vinegar

⅓ cup canola oil

¼ cup lemon juice

2 large garlic cloves, crushed

1 tablespoon salt

1 teaspoon poultry seasoning

1 teaspoon parsley flakes

½ teaspoon pepper

¼ cup honey (optional)

In a 2-cup liquid measuring cup, mix together marinade ingredients. Place chicken thighs in a bowl, add marinade, and toss. Cover and marinate in refrigerator for 6–12 hours. Grill until done (around 10 minutes per side, or until center reaches 165°F).

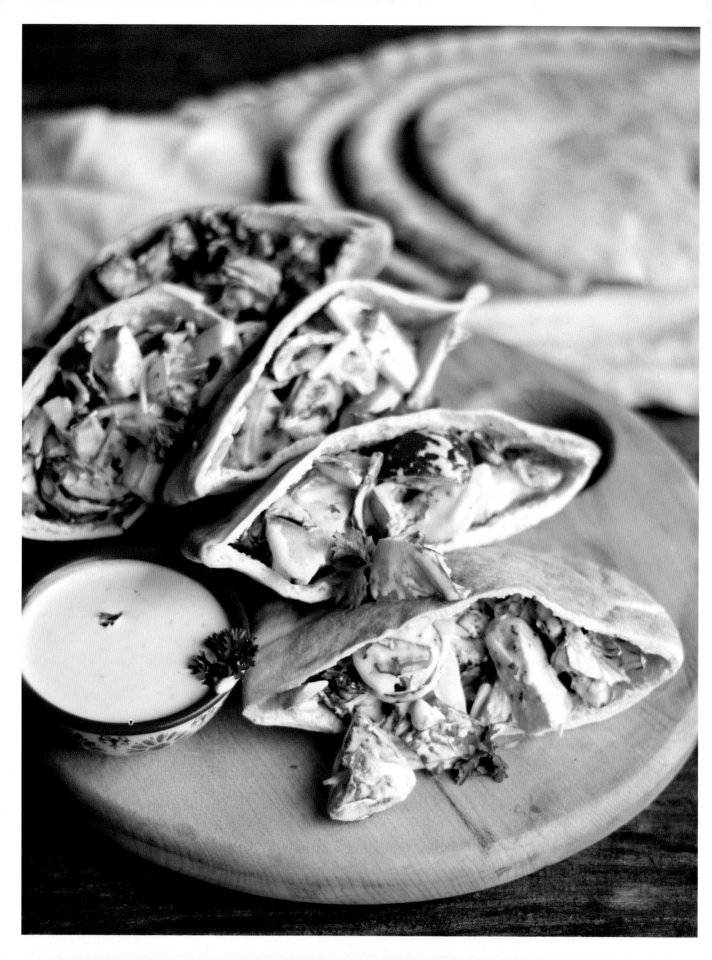

GRILLED CHICKEN PITAS

Serves 6

Grilled chicken pitas are great for an outdoor summer party. These pitas use a marinade recipe and a dressing recipe found elsewhere in this book. If you don't like blue cheese, you don't have to add the blue cheese crumbles. Joshua usually doesn't like blue cheese, but he actually enjoys eating it this way. You could also use this same recipe idea with a different dressing. And if you aren't serving these right away, skip tossing the meat and vegetables with the dressing and serve the dressing on the side.

marinade for Citrus Grilled Chicken (p. 197)

8 boneless, skinless chicken thighs

3 cups chopped fresh vegetables, such as:
 lettuce
 cucumbers
 green bell peppers
 tomatoes
 onions

1 cup Blue Cheese Dressing (p. 92)

½ cup shredded mozzarella cheese

6–7 rounds whole wheat pita bread

Combine marinade ingredients and marinate chicken thighs for 1 hour. Grill until done, then chop chicken into pieces.

In a bowl, mix together grilled chicken, vegetables, and shredded cheese.

In another bowl, mix together dressing ingredients. Pour 1 cup dressing over chicken, vegetables, and cheese, or just enough so that everything is lightly coated. Toss well. Refrigerate remaining dressing. It should keep for 10 days.

Slice pitas in half and stuff with filling. Makes 12–14 pita halves, depending how full you stuff them.

CORNMEAL-CRUSTED CHICKEN TENDERS

Serves 4

I like the flavor the cornmeal adds to these tenders. And of course, anything pan-fried in butter tastes good!

1 cup unbleached white flour

⅓ cup cornmeal

1 teaspoon salt

½ teaspoon pepper

1 egg

½ cup buttermilk

10 chicken tenders

¼ cup butter

In a pie pan, combine flour, cornmeal, salt, and pepper. In another pie pan, whisk together egg and buttermilk. Coat chicken tenders with egg mixture, then dredge in flour mixture.

Melt butter in skillet and add chicken tenders. Fry until golden brown, about 4 minutes per side. Serve with dipping sauce of your choice.

NOTE: These can be baked on a baking sheet lined with parchment paper. Spray or brush tops with canola oil and bake at 375°F for 15 minutes.

CRISPY CHICKEN NUGGETS

Serves 4

This recipe is super kid friendly, but we adults like it too! Serve with Honey Mustard Dressing (p. 93) and you'll have a winner.

---

canola oil

8 boneless, skinless chicken thighs

1 cup buttermilk

Breading

1 cup unbleached white flour

1 cup panko bread crumbs

1 teaspoon paprika

1 teaspoon poultry seasoning

1 tablespoon seasoned salt

½ teaspoon pepper

Line a baking sheet with parchment paper and coat well with canola oil. Mix together breading ingredients.

Cut chicken into 2-inch pieces. Dip chicken pieces in buttermilk (see tip below), then coat with breading. Place chicken on the baking sheet and spray or brush tops with canola oil. This helps make them crispy.

Bake at 375°F for 20–30 minutes, flipping halfway, or until juices run clear.

TIP: If I have time, I soak the chicken in the buttermilk in the refrigerator for 1–2 hours before coating with breading. Soaking in buttermilk ahead of time tenderizes the chicken through the actions of enzymes naturally present in buttermilk.

HONEY ROASTED CHICKEN

Serves 4

Here is a fuss-free way to make chicken for supper.

8 bone-in chicken thighs, skin
   removed

salt

Sauce

⅓ cup honey

¼ cup canola oil

2 teaspoons lemon juice

1 large garlic clove, crushed

1 teaspoon salt

½ teaspoon pepper

½ teaspoon rosemary

Lightly salt both sides of chicken thighs.

In a 2-cup liquid measuring cup, mix together sauce ingredients.

Lay chicken, bone up, in a 9 x 13-inch pan and pour sauce over it. Let stand for 1 hour. Bake at 375°F for 45 minutes, flipping chicken after 20 minutes.

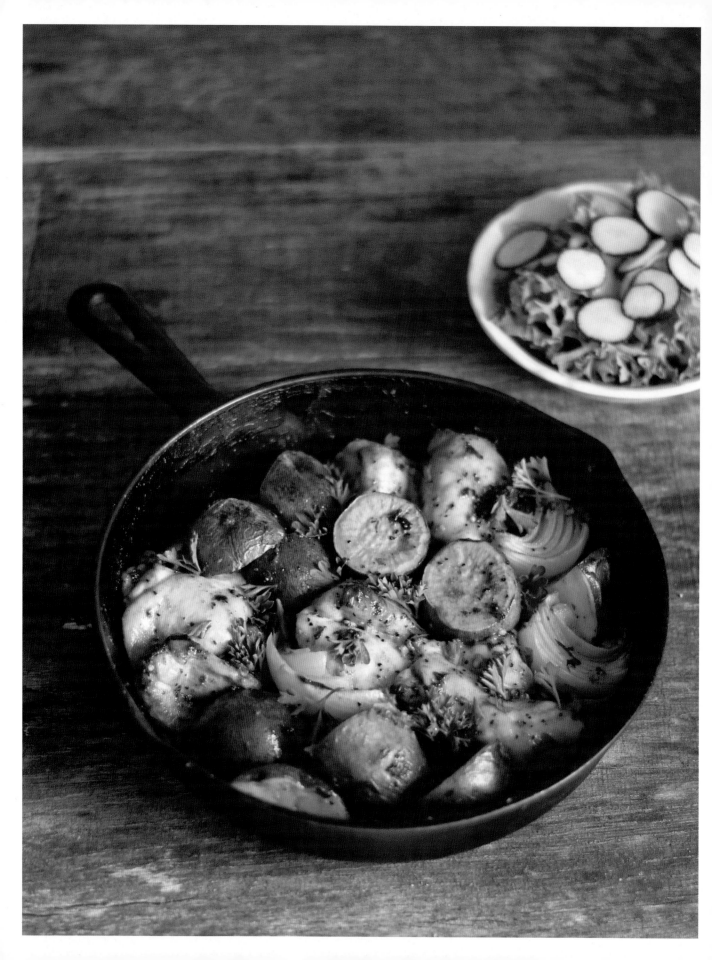

HERB ROASTED CHICKEN THIGHS AND POTATOES

Serves 4

An easy one-dish meal that is full of flavor and color. The chicken melts in your mouth.

---

8 boneless, skinless chicken thighs

1 onion, cut into chunks

1 sweet potato, cut into chunks

3 red potatoes, cut into chunks

Sauce

¼ cup butter

4 garlic cloves, crushed

1 teaspoon brown sugar

½ teaspoon salt

½ teaspoon pepper

½ teaspoon poultry seasoning

⅛–¼ teaspoon cayenne pepper

1 tablespoon chopped fresh parsley

Lay chicken and vegetables in a greased large skillet or a 9 x 13-inch baking dish.

Make sauce: In a small saucepan, melt butter and add garlic, brown sugar, salt, pepper, poultry seasoning, cayenne pepper, and parsley. Pour sauce over chicken and vegetables. Toss well with hands to make sure sauce is coated evenly. Bake at 350°F for 1½ hour.

WHOLE ROASTED CHICKEN

Serves 4–6

Roasting a whole chicken is so easy and can feed a family for two days. Save the leftover meat to make soup or chicken salad and the bones to make your own bone broth.

1 (5- to 6-pound) roasting chicken

1 lemon, halved

1 head garlic, cut in half crosswise

¼ cup butter, melted

paprika

salt

freshly ground black pepper

1 large onion, cut into chunks

4 carrots, cut into 2-inch pieces

olive oil

Remove giblets from chicken cavity and rinse chicken (discard giblets or use in another recipe). Pat chicken dry with a paper towel. Place in a roasting pan. Sprinkle salt and pepper inside cavity and insert half the lemon and head of garlic. Brush entire chicken liberally with butter and squeeze remaining lemon over chicken. Sprinkle all over with paprika, salt, and pepper.

Place the onions and carrots in the roasting pan around chicken. Drizzle with oil and sprinkle with salt and pepper. Roast, uncovered, at 425°F for 1½ hour, or until the juices run clear. The internal temperature should reach 165°F. You can cover halfway through to keep it from getting too brown. The skin will still get brown because of the paprika, but don't worry: it's not burnt but just full of flavor!

Remove from oven and let rest 10 minutes before serving.

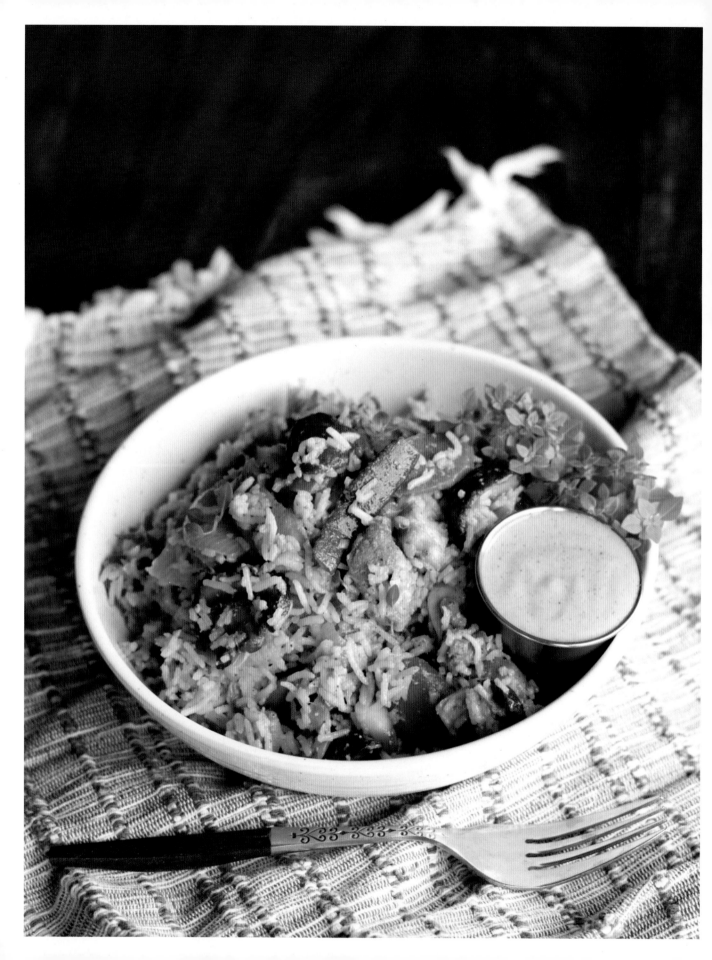

TERIYAKI CHICKEN AND FRIED RICE

Serves 4–6

My first date with Joshua was at a Japanese steakhouse. We both love Japanese food. Use the vegetable types and amounts in this recipe as a guide; personally, I like to use whatever vegetables are in season. I also use this recipe with leftover meats. Just add the leftover meat after your vegetables are tender.

2 cups uncooked basmati rice

2 tablespoons oil

8 chicken thighs, cut into strips

salt and pepper

1 tablespoon oil

1 medium onion, sliced

3 large carrots, sliced

1 medium zucchini, cut into matchsticks

10 fresh mushrooms, halved

2 eggs

Teriyaki sauce

2 garlic cloves, crushed

¼ teaspoon ginger paste, or 1 teaspoon freshly grated ginger

¼ cup soy sauce

¼ cup water

1 tablespoon rice vinegar

2 tablespoons granulated sugar

1 tablespoon brown sugar

2 teaspoons cornstarch

Yum yum sauce

1 cup mayonnaise

¼ cup ketchup

2 tablespoons granulated sugar

¼ teaspoon salt

⅛ teaspoon paprika

Cook rice according to package directions and set aside.

In a small saucepan, whisk together teriyaki sauce ingredients and cook until thickened. Set aside.

In a large skillet on medium heat, heat 2 tablespoons oil. When hot, add chicken strips. Sprinkle with salt and pepper. Fry until golden brown. Remove from skillet.

Add 1 tablespoon additional oil to the skillet and add the onions and carrots. (If vegetables start to stick, add a little water to loosen up the bottom.) Sauté until vegetables begin to get tender; then add zucchini and mushrooms. Sauté until all vegetables are tender. Stir in cooked rice.

Make a well in the middle of the rice mixture and crack open the eggs. Stir quickly and scramble into rice mixture. Add chicken and teriyaki sauce. Stir and fry for another 2–3 minutes. Season to taste with salt and pepper.

In a small bowl, mix together yum yum sauce ingredients and serve on the side.

TIP: This recipe is a great way to use up leftover rice.

CITRUS SHRIMP KABOBS

Serves 4–6

Citrus and Cajun flavors are wonderful on shrimp. I love grilling meats in the summer because it means less mess in the kitchen.

---

2 pounds raw shrimp, peeled

Sauce
½ cup orange marmalade
½ cup honey
1 tablespoon olive oil
2 tablespoons Cajun seasoning

In a small saucepan, combine sauce ingredients and bring to a boil. Remove from heat. Reserve ½ cup sauce to drizzle over shrimp before serving.

Thread shrimp on kabob sticks and baste with remaining sauce 1 hour before grilling.

Grill shrimp until pink and curled. Heat reserved sauce and drizzle over kabobs.

SHRIMP ALFREDO

Serves 4

A great meal for a special occasion, this dish goes well with steamed broccoli and a lettuce salad.

½ pound uncooked fettuccine

1 teaspoon salt

1 tablespoon olive oil

1 tablespoon butter

1 large garlic clove, crushed

1 pound raw shrimp, peeled

salt and pepper

Sauce

¼ cup white wine

1½ cup milk

½ cup half-and-half

1 tablespoon cornstarch

¼ teaspoon dried basil, or 1 tablespoon fresh basil

¼ cup freshly grated Parmesan
cheese

1 teaspoon lemon juice

Cook fettuccine with 1 teaspoon salt according to package directions. Strain and coat with olive oil. This helps keep the pasta from sticking together.

In a skillet, melt butter, add garlic, and sauté until fragrant. Add shrimp; sprinkle with salt and pepper. Cook until pink. Remove from skillet.

Add wine to the pan drippings and reduce to half. In a 2-cup or larger liquid measuring pitcher, whisk together milk, half-and-half, and cornstarch. Pour into skillet and simmer until thickened. Add basil and Parmesan cheese and stir until melted.

Return shrimp to skillet and simmer until shrimp are hot. Remove from heat and add lemon juice. Taste for salt and sprinkle a little in if you think it needs it. Serve over fettuccine.

CLASSIC STEAMED SHRIMP
with Cocktail Sauce
Serves 2–4

A classic way to fix shrimp. We have steamed shrimp every Christmas.

1 pound shrimp, unpeeled

2 cups water

2 cups white vinegar

¼ cup Old Bay seasoning

2 teaspoons salt

Cocktail sauce

¾ cup ketchup

2 teaspoons creamy horseradish

1 tablespoon lemon juice

½ teaspoon Worcestershire sauce

2 teaspoons brown sugar

¼ teaspoon salt

freshly ground pepper, to taste

In a small bowl, mix together cocktail sauce ingredients. Refrigerate until ready to serve.

Rinse shrimp. In a pot, heat water, vinegar, Old Bay seasoning, and salt until boiling. Add shrimp. Cover and cook 3 minutes, or until shrimp are pink. Serve immediately with cocktail sauce.

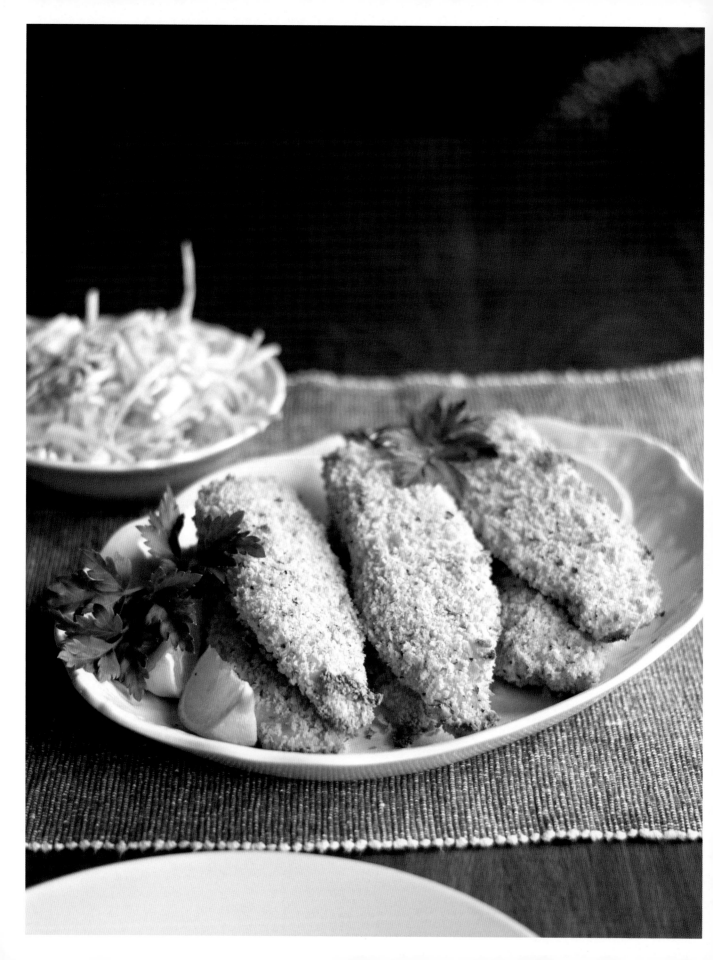

BAKED FISH

Serves 4

Baking fish instead of frying it saves you from cleaning up splattered oil. You can bread the fish when it's partially frozen and let it thaw until you are ready to bake it. I like to use flounder or tilapia in this recipe.

1 cup unbleached white flour
6 fish fillets

Egg wash
3 eggs, beaten
3 tablespoons water

Breading
2 cups panko bread crumbs
1 teaspoon dried dill
2 teaspoons salt
¼ teaspoon pepper

Set out three pie pans. Place flour in one. Whisk together egg wash in another. Mix together breading ingredients in the third pan. (It will be worth the mess, I promise!)

Coat fish with flour, then dip into egg wash, and then into breading. Place on a baking sheet lined with parchment paper and bake at 400°F for 20–22 minutes, until fish flakes easily with a fork, or internal temperature reaches 145°F. Serve with Tartar Sauce (p. 93).

Low Country Boil

Every July, around sweet corn season, we host several Low Country Boil suppers. Low Country Boil (p. 224), which originates in the South, usually consists of some type of shellfish, smoked sausage, new potatoes, corn on the cob, and onions.

We inherited Joshua's grandfather's copper kettle when we bought their house. (Shh . . . don't tell our family members.) It's been so much fun to use this kettle over a campfire to cook Low Country Boil. Sometimes, as I'm getting ready for a Low Country Boil supper, I wonder what other meals have been made in this old kettle. I make Cocktail Sauce (p. 95), in which we dip the shrimp and sausage, and serve sour cream to top the new potatoes. Of course, there is always plenty of butter, salt, and pepper for the sweet corn.

Low Country Boil is a fun, hands-on meal that includes filling your plate with the food that has been strewn down the middle of a table covered in newspaper. It took my mom a while to get used to the idea of using her hands to fill her plate. But now she digs in like the rest of us.

We serve our suppers down by the river that runs by the front of our property. The river helps cool the summer air, and the sound of running water adds a relaxing element. This meal has a way of making table conversations come easy. Eating with your fingers, serving ears of corn at your end of the table, and constantly passing butter, salt, and pepper has a way of bringing together everyone at the table.

This has been such a fun summer tradition. It feels like we are giving Grandfather's kettle more stories to tell.

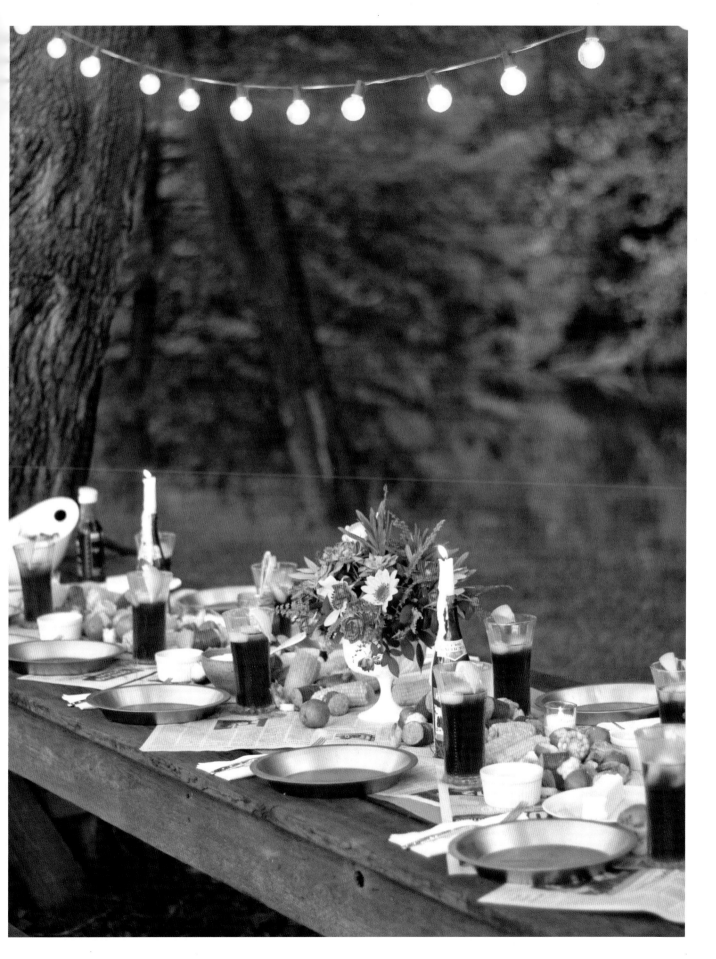

LOW COUNTRY BOIL

Serves 15

A perfect summer meal when sweet corn is just coming in. Low Country Boil is a great meal for larger groups. It can be done inside on the stove in a large pot or outside over a fire in a kettle.

1½ gallon water

¼ cup Old Bay seasoning

1 tablespoon salt

4 pounds small red potatoes

2 pounds kielbasa sausage, cut into 3-inch pieces

12 ears fresh corn, halved

4 large onions, cut into chunks

5 pounds raw shrimp

In a very large pot, add water, Old Bay seasoning, and salt. Bring to a hard boil; add potatoes and cook 10 minutes.

Add kielbasa to pot and cook 10 minutes more. Add corn and cook 3 minutes. Add onions and cook 2 minutes. Last, add shrimp and cook just until pink (around 3 minutes).

Using oven mitts and a large slotted spoon, dip the items out of the hot water and place in pans. Spread down the middle of a table covered in newspaper.

Serve with Cocktail Sauce (p. 95), sour cream, butter, salt, and pepper.

CRAB CAKES

Serves 2–4

There is nothing like a fresh fried crab cake! Top these with Tartar Sauce (p. 93). Be sure to buy lump crab meat and drain it well! If you don't drain off the liquid, the cakes will fall apart.

2 (6-ounce) cans lump crab meat

¾ cup crushed crackers

1 slice bread, crumbled

¼ cup chopped onion

¼ cup chopped green bell pepper

1 small garlic clove, minced

¼ cup mayonnaise

1 egg, beaten

1 teaspoon lemon juice

½ teaspoon Worcestershire sauce

½ teaspoon Dijon mustard

½ teaspoon Old Bay seasoning

½ teaspoon salt

dash cayenne pepper

unbleached white flour, for dusting

oil, for frying

Heat oven to 200°F.

With a strainer, drain crab meat well. Place crab meat in a medium bowl and add ingredients in order listed, up through cayenne pepper. Mix well. Form patties using ⅓ cup mixture per patty. Dust with flour.

In a deep skillet, add 2 inches of oil and heat on medium-high. Carefully drop crab cakes in oil and fry until brown on both sides (about 4 minutes per side). Rest on a plate lined with paper towels. Then place finished crab cakes on a baking dish in the oven to keep hot until serving.

Top with tartar sauce and serve.

SWEETS

I love sweets, but I don't always make fancy or exotic desserts. I tend to fall back on my old faithful recipes. I like to bake with whatever fruits are in season. As soon as spring hits, I'm looking forward to rhubarb and strawberry desserts. Come summertime, sour cherries are on my mind. When the cool air moves in, I start dreaming about apple dumplings and ice cream. Winter makes me want to sip hot drinks and nibble on scones and cookies.

Rhubarb Bars

Grandma's Rhubarb Crunch

Cobbler Cake

Strawberry Shortcake

Cream Cheese and Fruit Delight

Chocolate Cake
with Chocolate Buttercream Frosting

Autumn Apple Cake with Caramel Icing

Apple Cinnamon Shortbread Bars

Apple Dumplings

Caramel Apples

Caramel Custard

Pie Crust

Classic Fruit Pie

Fresh Strawberry Pie

Peanut Butter Pie

Maple Pecan Pie

Pumpkin Pie

Pumpkin Bars with Cream Cheese Frosting

Chocolate Zucchini Bars

Peanut Butter Bars

Granola Bars

Sugar Cookies

Chocolate Chip Cookies

Chewy Oatmeal Cookies

Glazed Doughnuts

Protein Balls

Three-Colored Coconut Candy

Peanut Butter Balls

Chocolate Bark

RHUBARB BARS

Serves 12

This is the first rhubarb recipe I make when my rhubarb is ready in early spring. This buttery cake, topped with a rhubarb filling, is what rhubarb lovers' dreams are made of.

---

1 cup butter, softened

1½ cup granulated sugar

3 eggs

3 cups unbleached white flour

1 teaspoon baking powder

½ teaspoon salt

1 teaspoon vanilla extract

Filling

1 cup water

1 cup granulated sugar

3 tablespoons cornstarch

3 tablespoons strawberry jam

1 teaspoon vanilla extract

4 cups chopped rhubarb

Glaze

⅓ cup powdered sugar

2 teaspoons cream

In a stand mixer fitted with the paddle attachment, cream butter and granulated sugar. Add eggs one at a time and mix well. Add flour, baking powder, salt, and vanilla. Line a 9 x 13-inch baking dish with parchment paper and spread three-quarters of the batter into the baking dish. The batter will be thick.

Make filling: In a saucepan, whisk together water, granulated sugar, and cornstarch. Heat until thickened, remove from heat, and add strawberry jam and vanilla. Add chopped rhubarb and stir. Pour rhubarb mixture over batter and top with remaining batter by adding spoonfuls evenly over the top. Smooth out batter, letting the filling show at some places. Bake at 325°F for 1 hour, or until a wooden pick inserted in the center comes out clean.

Remove from oven and cool completely. Mix together glaze ingredients and drizzle over bars before serving.

GRANDMA'S RHUBARB CRUNCH

Serves 8

A recipe from my grandma Shank that is timeless. Make sure to serve it warm with vanilla ice cream.

4 cups chopped rhubarb

Thickening

1 cup granulated sugar

1 cup water

2 tablespoons cornstarch

2 tablespoons strawberry jam

1 teaspoon vanilla extract

Crumbs

1 cup unbleached white flour

1 cup rolled oats

1 cup brown sugar

½ cup melted butter

1 teaspoon ground cinnamon

Make thickening: In a saucepan, whisk together granulated sugar, water, and cornstarch and cook until thickened. Remove from heat and add strawberry jam and vanilla. Mix in chopped rhubarb.

Make crumbs: In a medium bowl, mix together crumb ingredients and lightly press half the crumbs into a 9 x 9-inch baking dish. Top with rhubarb mixture. Cover with remaining crumbs. Bake at 350°F for 45 minutes. Serve warm with vanilla ice cream.

COBBLER CAKE

Serves 10

Cobbler cake is a great way to use fruit that is in season. Serve with fresh whipped cream or vanilla ice cream.

½ cup butter, softened

1½ cup sugar

4 eggs

2 teaspoons baking powder

1 teaspoon vanilla extract

¼ teaspoon salt

2 cups unbleached white flour

4 cups fruit, fresh or frozen

¼–½ cup sugar

In a stand mixer fitted with the paddle attachment, cream butter and 1½ cup sugar. Add eggs one at a time; then add baking powder, vanilla, salt, and flour in order listed. Mix just until combined.

Spread into a greased (or parchment paper–lined) 9 x 13-inch baking dish and top with fruit of your choice. Sprinkle top with ¼–½ cup sugar. (I gauge the amount by how sweet the fruit is.) Bake at 325°F for 1 hour, or until a wooden pick inserted in the middle comes out clean. Time will vary depending on fruit choice and whether it's fresh or frozen.

STRAWBERRY SHORTCAKE

Serves 8

I grew up eating this shortcake recipe. It's my grandma's recipe, revised just a little. Every spring, the first bite sure takes me back to my childhood. I love how food can hold memories.

½ cup butter, softened

½ cup sugar

1 egg

1 cup milk

2 cups unbleached white flour

3 teaspoons baking powder

½ teaspoon salt

1 teaspoon vanilla extract

In a medium bowl and using an electric hand mixer, cream butter and ½ cup sugar. Mix in egg. Add remaining ingredients and beat until just combined. Pour into a greased 9-inch skillet or baking pan. Sprinkle with a little additional sugar. Bake at 350°F for 25–30 minutes, or until a wooden pick inserted in the center comes out clean.

Serve with fresh strawberries and milk.

Strawberry season

Everyone in our home looks forward to strawberry season, but Caroline loves it the most. She loves to go along to my uncle's strawberry patch and help with the picking. I often say she should be weighed before and after she picks, so I can pay for how many she ate!

I grew up eating strawberry shortcake for many suppers in early summer. So in our early years of marriage, I made strawberry shortcake for supper one time, just the way Mom did. Feeling all nostalgic, I told Joshua how we used to eat this for supper as kids. "That's a touching story," he replied. "But, um, is this really all I'm eating for supper?" I had to laugh. I pulled some leftovers with meat in them out of the fridge. He ate dessert first that evening. I guess that tradition won't be carried on in our home—I haven't tried making strawberry shortcake for supper since.

When strawberries are in season, I usually pick them several times so we can eat them fresh. They don't keep long, and even a day after they are picked they aren't the same. I've found they do keep longer if you don't wash them and place them in a sealed container lined with paper towels.

The first strawberry dessert I usually make to kick off strawberry season is Fresh Strawberry Pie (p. 255). There is nothing like that first bite of flakey crust, piled high with fresh berries in a sweet glaze and topped with fresh whipped cream. Then I like to make Strawberry Shortcake (p. 234)—for dessert, of course! My mamma's recipe for shortcake is the best. It's an old-fashioned biscuit-type shortcake that's not too sweet. And I also love to make strawberry freezer jam. That way we can spread bread with strawberry jam in the middle of winter. That way we can be transplanted, just for a moment, to those lovely June days.

CREAM CHEESE AND FRUIT DELIGHT

Serves 12

Desserts like this one seem to always grace potluck tables. Like lots of other people, I love them too. The crunchy layer, the fluffy cream layer, and then the fruit layer: they're hard to beat. This is a nice dessert for a larger group and a great way to use seasonal fruits. Take your pick of graham, shortbread, or pretzel crust.

Fruit topping of your choice (see instructions)

Graham crust

½ cup butter, melted

2½ cups crushed graham cracker crumbs (2 packs)

2 tablespoons granulated sugar

Shortbread crust

1½ cup unbleached white flour

¼ cup granulated sugar

½ cup cold butter, grated

⅛ teaspoon baking powder

⅛ teaspoon baking soda

½ cup chopped pecans

Pretzel crust

¾ cup butter, melted

2 cups crushed pretzels

3 tablespoons sugar

Cream cheese filling

1 (8-ounce) package cream cheese, softened

½ cup powdered sugar

1 teaspoon vanilla extract

dash salt

1 pint (2 cups) heavy cream

For fruit topping: Prepare fresh glazed fruit or prepared pie filling of your choice. You can use the fruit filling for Classic Fruit Pie (p. 252). If so, add 1 cup crushed fresh fruit to the filling mixture before cooking until thickened. Remove from heat and cool to room temperature, then fold in 2 cups fresh fruit. Cool completely before spreading on top of cream cheese filling.

For graham crust: In a small bowl, mix together ingredients with a fork and press firmly into a 9 x 13-inch baking dish. Freeze until firm.

For shortbread crust: In a small bowl, mix together flour and granulated sugar and cut in butter. Add remaining ingredients. Press into a 9 x 13-inch baking dish and bake at 350°F for 12 minutes. Let cool completely.

For pretzel crust: In a small bowl, mix together ingredients with a fork. Press firmly into a 9 x 13-inch baking dish and bake at 350°F for 10 minutes. Let cool completely.

Make cream cheese filling: Using a stand mixer fitted with the wire whip, beat cream cheese and powdered sugar until smooth. Add vanilla and salt. Slowly pour in heavy cream and beat on medium-high for 2 minutes, or until stiff peaks form. Spread over cooled crust.

TIP: This recipe makes 5 cups of cream cheese filling. This filling can be used as a light icing on a cake or as a cream filling for a cake trifle.

CHOCOLATE CAKE
with Chocolate Buttercream Frosting
Makes 1 (9-inch round) layer cake

I've made this chocolate cake for years. Joshua asks for this every time his birthday comes around. He never seems to get tired of it. It is very moist, so it's very important to line the cake pan with parchment paper. Sometimes I add fresh fruit on top for a colorful garnish, along with chocolate curls.

2 cups unbleached white flour

2 cups sugar

½ cup cocoa powder

1½ teaspoon baking soda

1 teaspoon baking powder

1 teaspoon salt

1 cup oil

1 cup buttermilk

2 eggs

1 teaspoon vanilla extract

¾ cup hot espresso or strong coffee

Using a stand mixer fitted with the wire whip, mix together ingredients in order listed. (I usually have the mixer on low the whole time I mix up this cake.) Line two (9-inch round) cake pans with parchment paper and spray with baking spray (or use grease and flour). Pour batter equally between the two pans. Bake at 350°F for 30–35 minutes. Do not open the oven door before 30 minutes or the cake may fall. The cake is done when little cracks start appearing on the surface.

Cool 10 minutes, flip onto parchment paper, and lay on cooling rack.

Chocolate buttercream frosting

½ cup butter

2 cups powdered sugar

½ cup cocoa powder

½ teaspoon vanilla extract

dash salt

¼ cup milk

Remove butter from the refrigerator 30 minutes before starting. (You want it to be room temperature but not too soft.)

Using a stand mixer fitted with the wire whip, add butter to bowl and beat until smooth. Add powdered sugar, cocoa powder, vanilla, salt, and milk. Beat until fluffy (about 2 minutes). After cake is cooled, frost between layers and on top. Refrigerate cake immediately after spreading on frosting.

TIP: I usually make this cake ahead of time and freeze it; I wait to frost the cake until after it partially thaws. If you prefer a white icing, use the cream cheese filling for Cream Cheese and Fruit Delight (p. 239). If I use that for frosting, I add sliced fresh fruit between the layers and garnish the top.

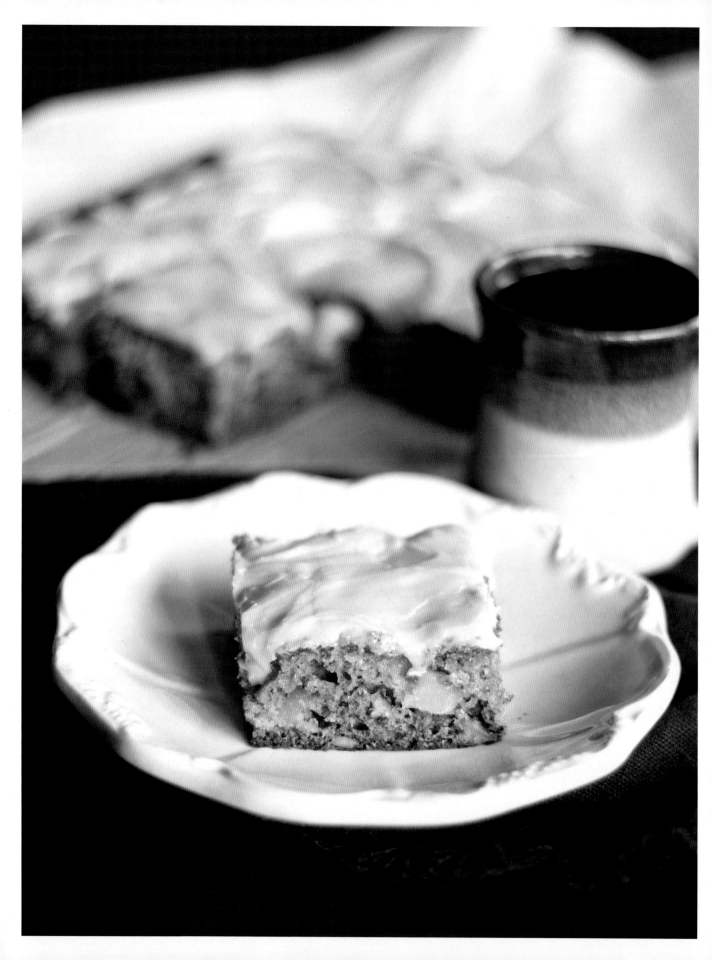

AUTUMN APPLE CAKE
with Caramel Icing
Makes 1 (9 x 13-inch) cake

Every fall I can't wait to make this cake. It's quick to make and can be mixed by hand.

4 cups peeled and chopped apples

1 cup sugar

2 eggs, beaten

½ cup butter, melted

2 cups unbleached white flour

2 teaspoons baking soda

¾ teaspoon salt

1 teaspoon ground cinnamon

¼ teaspoon ground ginger

¼ teaspoon ground nutmeg

1 cup chopped pecans

In a medium bowl, mix together apples and sugar. Let stand for a few minutes, or until apples release juices. Add eggs and melted butter and mix until combined. In another bowl, mix together flour, baking soda, salt, cinnamon, ginger, nutmeg, and pecans. Add flour mixture to apple mixture and mix until combined. Spread into greased 9 x 13-inch baking dish and bake at 325°F for 35 minutes, or until cake tester or wooden pick inserted in the center comes out clean.

Caramel icing

¼ cup butter

⅓ cup brown sugar

⅛ teaspoon salt

2 tablespoons milk

1 cup powdered sugar

½ teaspoon vanilla extract

In a small saucepan, melt butter and then stir in brown sugar and salt. Cook, stirring, until the sugar melts. Add the milk, bring to a boil, and pour into a mixing bowl to cool for 10 minutes.

After 10 minutes, stir in the powdered sugar and vanilla. Whisk until smooth. Spread on warm cake.

APPLE CINNAMON SHORTBREAD BARS

Makes 12 bars

I love shortbread crusts. The cinnamon cream cheese paired with the sugared apples makes a delightful harmony of fall flavors. I use Gala apples in this recipe.

Crust

¼ cup chopped pecans

1½ cup unbleached white flour

¼ cup granulated sugar

⅛ teaspoon baking powder

⅛ teaspoon baking soda

½ cup butter, melted

Filling

1 (8-ounce) package cream cheese, softened

¼ cup brown sugar

½ teaspoon ground cinnamon

1 teaspoon vanilla extract

Apple topping

2–3 apples, peeled and sliced

2 tablespoons granulated sugar

¼ teaspoon ground cinnamon

Make crust: In a small bowl, combine crust ingredients. Firmly press into a 9 x 13-inch baking dish and set aside.

Make filling: In a medium bowl and with an electric mixer, beat together filling ingredients until smooth. Carefully spread over crust. (Start with small spoonfuls all over the crust to prevent the crust from pulling up while spreading. An angled spatula works best.)

Layer apple slices evenly on top of the cream cheese filling. In a small bowl, combine granulated sugar and cinnamon. Sprinkle over apples. Bake at 350°F for 35–40 minutes, or until apples are tender. Let cool completely before cutting into squares and serving. Refrigerate after serving.

TIP: You can also make this recipe in a 10-inch springform pan. It's a more elegant version for guests. I've used pears for the top as well.

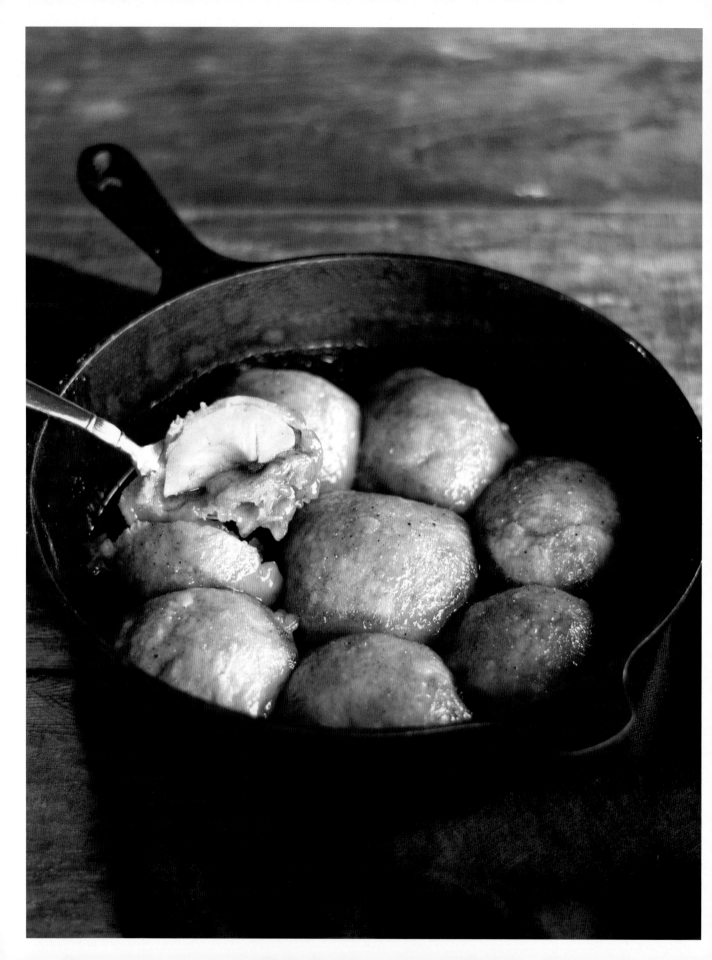

APPLE DUMPLINGS

Makes 14 dumplings

Apple dumplings are like little packages of fall. There is something special about them; maybe it's the time and effort you know someone put into making them. Gala apples are perfect for this recipe.

1 double-crust pie dough (p. 251)
7 apples, peeled, halved, and cored
brown sugar
ground cinnamon
butter

Sauce
1 cup granulated sugar
1 cup brown sugar
3 cups water
½ teaspoon ground cinnamon
½ teaspoon ground nutmeg
¼ cup butter

Divide dough in half. Roll one half into a 14 x 18-inch rectangle. Lay half the apples on top of the dough, cut side up and spaced apart. Cut squares of dough around them with a knife, just large enough to cover the apple. (Cut one square and see if you are guessing the size right.)

Fill each apple center with a rounded teaspoon of brown sugar and a dash cinnamon. Top with a small dab of butter. Fold ends of dough squares to the center of the apple and pinch edges together. Place in a 9 x 13-inch baking dish with the flat side down. Repeat with remaining half of dough and apples, placing in a second baking dish.

In a saucepan, combine sauce ingredients except for butter. Heat to boiling. Remove from heat and add butter.

Divide sauce in half and pour over each baking dish of apple dumplings. Bake at 375°F for 35 minutes. Serve warm with ice cream.

CARAMEL APPLES

Makes 16 apples

I've made big batches of these caramel apples to sell for a few fall events in our area. Now, at home, it's fun to make 16 instead of 200!

---

16 small apples

16 wooden sticks

Caramel

2¼ cups brown sugar

½ cup butter

1 cup dark corn syrup

1 (14-ounce) can sweetened condensed milk

¼ teaspoon salt

1 teaspoon vanilla extract

Wash apples and dry well. Push a wooden stick into each apple center.

In a heavy saucepan, combine all caramel ingredients except vanilla. Cook over medium heat until sugar dissolves. Increase heat and cook, stirring constantly, until mixture reaches 240°F on a candy thermometer. Remove from heat and cool to 200°F. Stir in vanilla. Quickly dip apples in caramel sauce and place on greased parchment paper. Place in freezer until hardened. Place in bags and store in refrigerator. Good for up to 1 week.

CARAMEL CUSTARD

Serves 16

When I was growing up, we often served this silky custard when company came to our home.

1¼ cup brown sugar

½ cup butter

2 tablespoons cold water

7½ cups milk, divided

3 eggs, beaten

⅔ cup cornstarch

½ cup unbleached white flour

1 teaspoon salt

1 tablespoon unflavored gelatin

¼ cup water

2 teaspoons vanilla extract

In a skillet, caramelize brown sugar and butter until fragrant. Remove from heat. Add cold water and stir until smooth.

Pour 7 cups milk into a large saucepan. Whisk in the caramel mixture, stirring constantly, and heat to almost boiling.

In a 2-cup liquid measuring cup, whisk together remaining ½ cup milk, eggs, cornstarch, flour, and salt until smooth. Add to hot milk mixture while stirring, and heat until thickened. Remove from heat.

Dissolve gelatin in ¼ cup water. Add dissolved gelatin and vanilla to custard. Blend with an immersible blender and then refrigerate until set. Before serving, whip with an electric hand mixer until smooth.

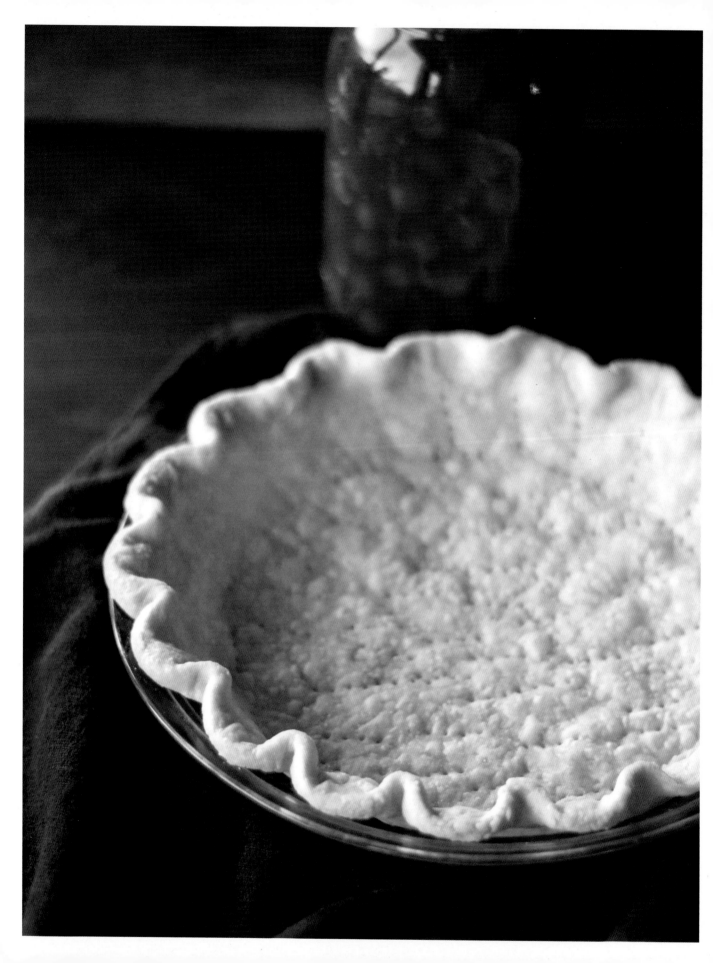

PIE CRUST

Makes 2 deep-dish pie crusts

Here's my favorite pie crust recipe, which makes either two pies (bottom crust only) or one pie (with a top crust). Making pie crust is often viewed as complicated. But if you've only tried it once or twice, don't give up just yet. Practice makes perfect. You will learn helpful techniques the more often you make pie crust. My tips? Do not add too much water and do not overwork the dough.

2½ cups unbleached white flour

1 teaspoon salt

10 tablespoons cold butter

¼ cup cold lard (or shortening)

8–10 tablespoons ice water (approximately)

In a stand mixer fitted with the paddle attachment, mix together flour and salt. Grate butter and return to the refrigerator. Measure the lard and get the ice water ready. Remove butter from the refrigerator.

Start mixer on medium speed. Add lard in small spoonfuls, then add grated butter in small handfuls. Mix until the biggest butter clump is the size of a large pea. Remove bowl from mixer stand. (You can also do this step with a hand pastry blender.)

Using a fork to gently mix dough, add water 1 tablespoon at a time. Important: As soon as you see the dough come together, stop adding water. You can press it together with your hands and see if it stays together. It's okay if there are some dry clumps in the bottom of the bowl. Dump dough on the counter and work it until it stays together, adding tiny amounts of water if needed.

Form dough into two rounds. Refrigerate for 1–2 hours before rolling out into two large circles and placing in pie pans. Cut edges and crimp as you desire.

If you are baking the crust before filling it, prick crust all over with a fork to let the heat escape. Carefully line your pie shell with foil to help hold the sides up while baking. Bake at 375°F for 8 minutes. Remove foil and bake 10 minutes more. If crust starts to bubble up, prick with a fork until bubbles deflate, then continue baking.

CLASSIC FRUIT PIE

Makes 1 (9-inch) pie

This recipe can be used with almost any fruit, fresh or frozen. I have found that if you use frozen fruit, the fruit still tastes really fresh.

1 (9-inch) unbaked pie shell

Fruit filling

1 cup water

¾ cup sugar

¼ cup Clear Jel

¼ teaspoon salt

1 teaspoon almond flavoring, or 1 tablespoon lemon juice

3–4 cups cut fruit (4 cups for a deep-dish pie)

Crumbs

⅓ cup unbleached white flour

¼ cup sugar

3 tablespoons cold butter, grated

In a small saucepan, mix water, sugar, Clear Jel, and salt. Cook until thickened. Remove from heat. Add almond flavoring or lemon juice, depending which you think tastes best with the fruit you are using. Fold in fruit and pour into unbaked pie shell.

For crumbs, in a small bowl mix together flour and sugar. Cut in butter until crumbs form. Sprinkle evenly on top of pie. Bake at 350°F for 45–55 minutes.

TIP: Here is a great way to know your fruit pie is done: the filling needs to bubble for at least 6–10 minutes to properly cook the fruit.

FRESH STRAWBERRY PIE

Makes 2 (9-inch) pies

Every time strawberry season came around during my childhood, we all eagerly anticipated this pie.

2 (9-inch) pie shells, baked

Fruit filling
2 cups water
¾ cup granulated sugar
3 tablespoons Clear Jel
dash salt
1 (3-ounce) box strawberry gelatin
10 cups sliced fresh strawberries

Whipped cream
1 pint (2 cups) heavy cream
½ cup powdered sugar
½ teaspoon vanilla extract
pinch salt

Make filling: In a small saucepan, stir together water, granulated sugar, Clear Jel, and salt. Cook until thickened. Remove from heat and add strawberry gelatin. Let cool to room temperature and add sliced strawberries. Pour into two baked pie shells and refrigerate until set.

Make whipped cream: In a medium bowl and using an electric mixer, beat together whipped cream ingredients until peaks form. Dollop on pies before serving.

PEANUT BUTTER PIE

Makes 1 (9-inch) pie

My mom is known far and wide for her peanut butter pie. Topped with fluffy whipped cream and clusters of peanut butter crumbs, this silky custard pie boasts the perfect textures.

---

1 (9-inch) pie shell, baked

Custard
2½ cups milk, divided

⅓ cup granulated sugar

¼ cup cornstarch

¼ cup unbleached white flour

¼ teaspoon salt

3 eggs yolks, beaten

2 teaspoons gelatin

¼ cup cold water

1 tablespoon butter

1 teaspoon vanilla extract

Crumbs
¾ cup powdered sugar

½ cup peanut butter

Whipped cream
1 pint (2 cups) heavy cream

½ cup powdered sugar

½ teaspoon vanilla extract

pinch salt

Make custard: In a double boiler, heat 2 cups milk until steamy. In a small bowl, combine remaining ½ cup milk with sugar, cornstarch, flour, and salt. Whisk until smooth or blend with an immersible blender. While stirring milk on stove, pour in this thickening mixture. Stir constantly and cook until custard is thickened.

Temper eggs by stirring a small amount of hot custard into egg yolks. Stirring constantly, add yolk mixture to hot custard and cook for about 3 minutes. Remove from heat.

Dissolve gelatin in ¼ cup cold water. Add butter, vanilla, and dissolved gelatin to hot custard. Stir well. Refrigerate until set; it will be very stiff.

Make crumbs: In a small bowl, mix peanut butter and powdered sugar until crumbs form. Refrigerate until ready to use.

Several hours before serving, whip custard with a hand mixer until smooth. Sprinkle about two-thirds of the crumbs into the baked pie shell. Reserve the remaining crumbs. Pour whipped custard over crumbs in pie shell. Return to the refrigerator for several hours so custard can set again.

Make whipped cream: In a medium bowl and using an electric mixer, beat together whipped cream ingredients until stiff peaks form. Spread on pie. Garnish pie with remaining peanut butter crumbs.

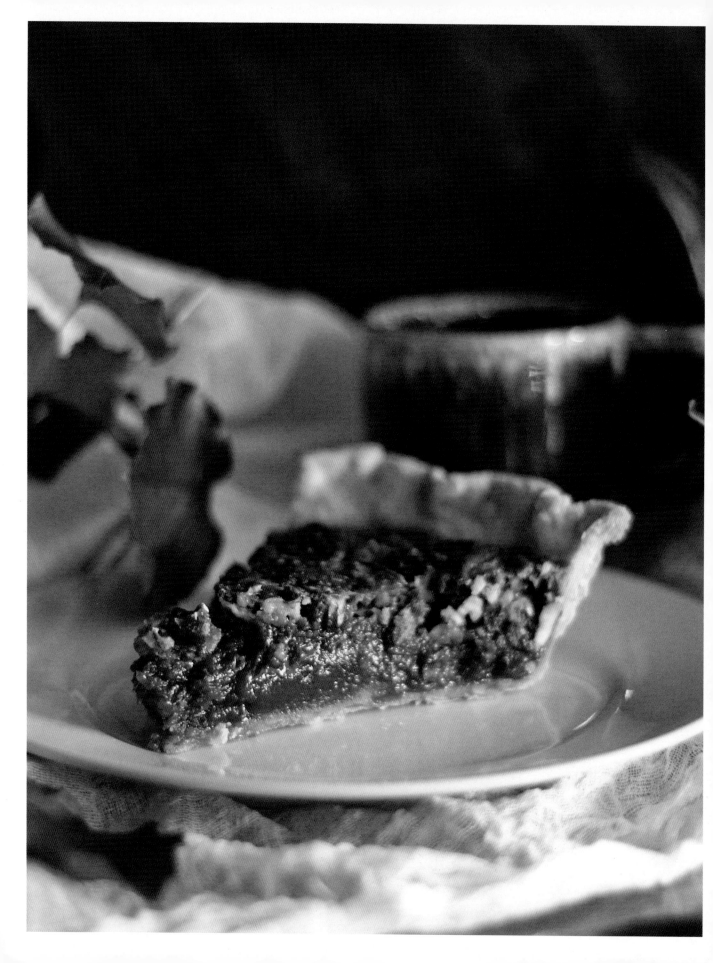

MAPLE PECAN PIE

Makes 1 (9-inch) pie

I love this recipe because it uses maple syrup instead of corn syrup. The whiskey is optional, and it adds another layer of flavor.

1 (9-inch) unbaked pie shell

Filling

1 cup maple syrup

1 tablespoon whiskey (optional)

3 large eggs

3 tablespoons butter, melted

1 teaspoon vanilla bean paste or vanilla extract

¾ cup brown sugar

2 tablespoons unbleached white flour

¼ teaspoon salt

1½ cup chopped pecans

In a bowl, whisk together all filling ingredients except the pecans. Place pecans in unbaked pie shell and pour syrup mixture over pecans. Bake at 350°F for 45–50 minutes, or until top starts to puff up and center seems set.

PUMPKIN PIE

Makes 1 (9-inch) pie

This is my mom's pumpkin pie recipe, which she originally got from a neighbor. This pie has been present at every Thanksgiving meal for as long as I can remember.

1 (9-inch) unbaked pie shell

Filling
2 eggs

½ cup milk

½ cup cream

1½ cup pumpkin puree

½ cup brown sugar

½ teaspoon salt

1 teaspoon ground cinnamon

½ teaspoon ground ginger

¼ teaspoon ground cloves

1 teaspoon vanilla extract

Blend all filling ingredients in a blender and pour into unbaked pie shell. Bake at 400°F for 15 minutes, reduce heat to 350°F, and bake 30 minutes more, or until center registers 175°F. The center will still be wobbly but will set as it cools. You can also insert a knife about 1 inch away from the crust's edge; if it comes out clean, it's done.

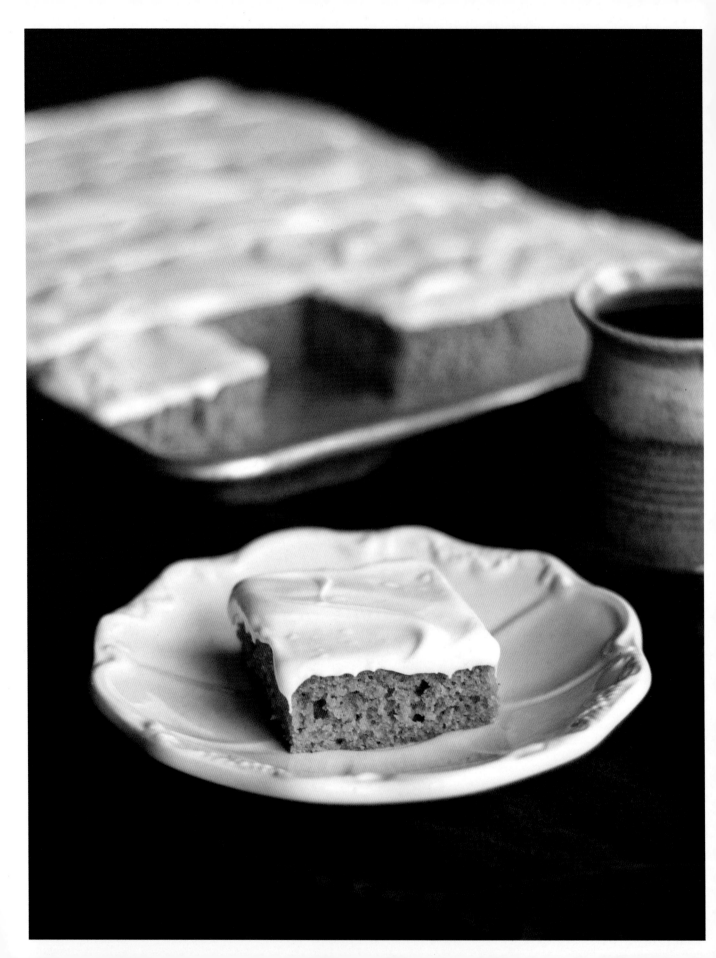

PUMPKIN BARS WITH CREAM CHEESE FROSTING

Makes 20 bars

This recipe from my grandma Shank is great for fall parties. Mom used to make these for our youth group parties, and she would top each square with a candy pumpkin.

1 cup oil

2 cups granulated sugar

4 eggs, beaten

2 cups pumpkin puree

2 teaspoons salt

2 teaspoons ground cinnamon

1 teaspoon baking soda

1 teaspoon baking powder

2 cups unbleached white flour

1 teaspoon vanilla extract

Frosting

1 (8-ounce) package cream cheese, softened

¼ cup butter, softened

2½ cups powdered sugar

1 teaspoon vanilla extract

dash salt

In a medium bowl and using an electric mixer, mix together batter ingredients in order listed. Pour batter into a greased and floured 13 x 18-inch baking sheet. Bake at 350°F for 20–25 minutes.

Make frosting: In a small bowl, use an electric mixer to beat together cream cheese and butter until smooth. Add powdered sugar, vanilla, and salt. Beat until fluffy and smooth. Spread on cooled bars.

CHOCOLATE ZUCCHINI BARS

Serves 12

These bars are a great way to use up zucchini, that overabundant garden vegetable. There are no eggs in this recipe. These are so good with a cold glass of milk.

2 cups shredded zucchini

1½ cup sugar

½ cup oil

2 cups unbleached white flour

½ cup cocoa powder

1½ teaspoon baking soda

1 teaspoon salt

In a large bowl, mix together zucchini, sugar, and oil. Add remaining ingredients and mix well. Spread into a greased 9 x 13-inch baking dish. Bake at 350°F for 30 minutes. Cool and then spread with ganache frosting.

Whipped ganache frosting

½ cup heavy cream

1 cup semisweet chocolate chips

In a small saucepan, heat heavy cream and chocolate chips until smooth. Refrigerate until just chilled but not stiff. With an electric mixer, beat until peaks form. Spread on cooled bars. Refrigerate after serving.

PEANUT BUTTER BARS

Makes about 20 bars

I have a hard time not eating these bars when they are present in my kitchen. The marriage of chocolate and peanut butter makes them irresistible.

---

1 cup butter, softened

¾ cup granulated sugar

¾ cup brown sugar

2 eggs

½ cup peanut butter

1 teaspoon salt

1 teaspoon baking soda

1 teaspoon vanilla extract

2 cups unbleached white flour

2 cups rolled oats

Topping

1 cup semisweet chocolate chips

½ cup peanut butter

Using a stand mixer fitted with the paddle attachment, cream butter, granulated sugar, and brown sugar. Add eggs and peanut butter and beat until fluffy. Add remaining batter ingredients and mix until just combined. Spread out batter evenly on a greased 13 x 18-inch baking sheet. Bake at 350°F for 15–18 minutes, or just until starting to brown at the edges. Do not overbake.

In a small saucepan (or a bowl in the microwave for 30 seconds), melt chocolate chips. Stir in peanut butter. Spread on top of warm bars, then refrigerate until chocolate is set. Cut into squares and enjoy!

GRANOLA BARS

Makes about 15 bars

These granola bars make a great snack or item for packed lunches. Children can help make them too.

4½ cups crispy rice cereal

2 cups rolled oats

9 graham crackers, crushed

½ cup chopped pecans

½ cup dried cranberries

½ cup shredded sweetened coconut

2 tablespoons wheat germ

¼ teaspoon salt

¼ cup butter

1 (10½-ounce) bag mini marshmallows

¼ cup honey

¼ cup peanut butter

½ cup chocolate chips

In a large bowl, mix together crispy rice cereal, rolled oats, crushed graham crackers, chopped pecans, cranberries, coconut, wheat germ, and salt.

In a saucepan, melt butter and marshmallows. Remove from heat and add honey and peanut butter. Pour melted mixture over cereal mixture, stirring constantly. Once everything sticks together, press mixture evenly into a greased 13 x 18-inch baking sheet. Sprinkle chocolate chips on top of bars. Top with a piece of greased waxed paper and roll with a rolling pin to press chocolate chips into mixture (this step avoids mixing the chocolate chips into the hot marshmallow mixture, which would cause the chocolate to melt). Cut into rectangles.

Christmas cookie bake

Every December my family has an annual "Christmas cookie bake." I started this tradition when I still lived at home. My best friend and I came up with the idea, and we ended up including all the relatives connected to our family farm.

Each lady brings her own big bowl of homemade cookie dough to Mom's house. Then we bake our cookies there together and each take home an assortment. We talk beforehand, to make sure everyone is making a different kind of cookie. You can always plan on Aunt Shirley making her famous chocolate crinkles. I usually make a classic cookie, and have started sprinkling a little fleur de sel (fancy sea salt) on top of each cookie before baking, as it adds a special touch.

It's so wonderful to almost have my Christmas cookie baking done in one day! I return home with nine plates of different Christmas cookies. On most Christmas cookie bake days we bake around fifteen hundred cookies. Then all I make at home for Christmas are Sugar Cookies (p. 273), Three-Colored Coconut Candy (p. 284), Peanut Butter Balls (p. 287), and Chocolate Bark (p. 288). I give our neighbors cookie plates and boxes of homemade candies as gifts.

If you were a mouse in a corner on a Christmas cookie bake day, you would hear chatting as cookies are scooped and placed on trays. You would see children peeking over the long table, eyeing rows of cooling cookies and hoping to get a sample. You would see Grandma sitting in an armchair, quietly taking in all the activity around. A Christmas cookie bake is not just about baking large amounts of cookies. It's about fellowship and community.

SUGAR COOKIES

Makes 8–9 dozen depending on cookie cutter size

When I think of Christmas cookies, I think of these sugar cookies. Mom would make them every year. I still remember opening the squeaky door of our chest freezer to sneak one to eat with Dad's hot chocolate.

1½ cup butter, softened

2 cups granulated sugar

6 egg yolks

1 cup sour cream

1 teaspoon vanilla extract

2 teaspoons baking powder

1½ teaspoon baking soda

1 teaspoon salt

6 cups unbleached white flour

Icing

1 cup butter, softened

1 teaspoon vanilla extract

⅛ teaspoon salt

1 egg yolk (optional)

6 cups powdered sugar

Make cookies: In a stand mixer fitted with the paddle attachment, cream butter and granulated sugar. Add egg yolks, sour cream, and vanilla. In another bowl, sift together baking powder, baking soda, salt, and flour. Add to egg mixture and mix just until combined. Refrigerate for 2 hours. Roll out dough ¼ inch thick and cut into shapes. Bake at 350°F for 8–10 minutes. Do not allow to brown. Cool completely before icing.

Make icing: In a stand mixer fitted with the wire whip, cream butter, vanilla, salt, and egg yolk, if desired. Add powdered sugar and beat until creamy. Add a little milk if the icing seems too thick. Ice cookies. If you don't plan to serve them right away, freeze to keep fresh.

CHOCOLATE CHIP COOKIES

Makes 4–5 dozen

This is the only cookie recipe my husband asks me to make. He claims there is no other cookie like this one. I freeze them in small bags for him to take to work for lunch. If you don't have lard, you can replace that ingredient with ½ cup butter instead.

½ cup butter, softened

½ cup lard

1 cup granulated sugar

1 cup brown sugar

3 eggs

2 teaspoons baking powder

2 teaspoons baking soda

2 teaspoons vanilla extract

½ teaspoon salt

3½ cups unbleached white flour

1 cup semisweet chocolate chips

Using a stand mixer fitted with the paddle attachment, cream butter, lard, granulated sugar, and brown sugar. Add remaining ingredients in order listed and mix just until combined.

Using a 1½-inch cookie scoop, scoop onto a baking sheet lined with parchment paper. Bake at 350°F for 8–9 minutes, or just until the tops are starting to brown. The cookies will look a little wet, but as they cool, they will become chewy and just right.

TIP: It's always good to bake two to three cookies for a test bake before baking the whole batch. That way, if your cookies fall flat, you have time to work in a little more flour before baking the rest.

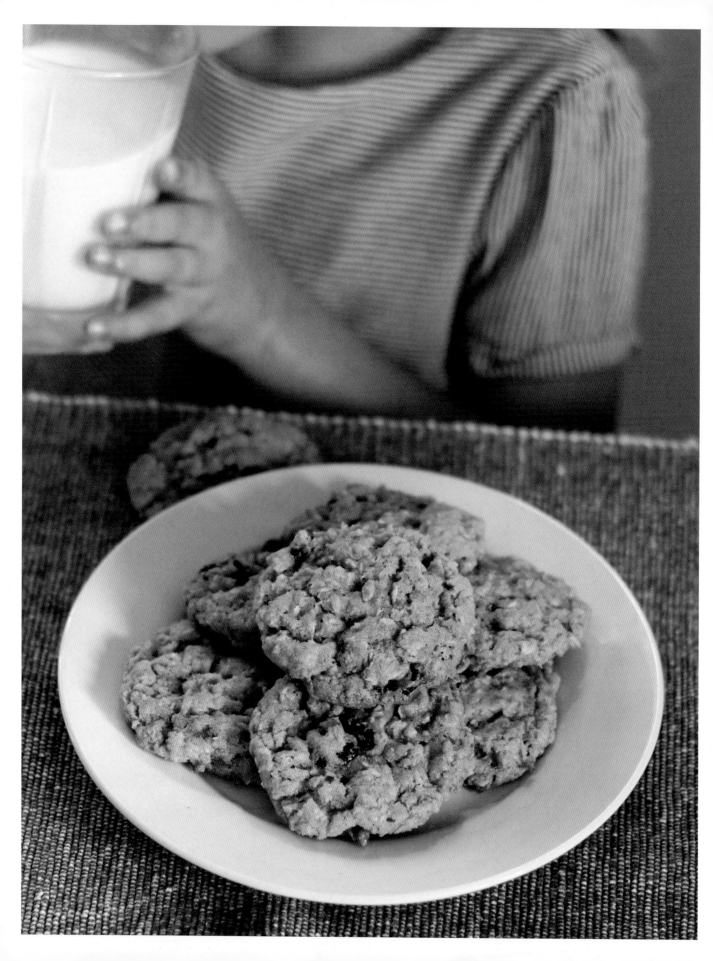

CHEWY OATMEAL COOKIES

Makes about 5 dozen

I don't make lots of different kinds of cookies; I'd rather have a couple of favorites. That way, deciding which kind of cookies to make is simple! These are the "other cookie" I make, besides chocolate chip. They are delightfully crunchy and chewy at the same time. Be sure to use rolled oats; quick oats will make a dry cookie. If you don't have lard, you can replace that ingredient with ½ cup butter instead.

½ cup butter, softened

½ cup lard

1 cup brown sugar

1 cup granulated sugar

2 eggs

1 teaspoon baking soda

1 teaspoon ground cinnamon

1 teaspoon vanilla extract

½ teaspoon salt

¾ cup raisins or dried cranberries

4 cups rolled oats

1 cup unbleached white flour

½ cup shredded sweetened coconut

Using a stand mixer fitted with the paddle attachment, cream butter, lard, brown sugar, and granulated sugar. Add remaining ingredients in order listed and mix until just combined. Refrigerate dough for 1 hour.

Using a 1½-inch cookie scoop, scoop onto a baking sheet lined with parchment paper. Bake at 350°F for 10–11 minutes. Underbaked, they fall flat; overbaked, they aren't as chewy. I find that 11 minutes is perfect. Even if they seem a little wet, they will set up once they cool.

GLAZED DOUGHNUTS

Makes 6–7 dozen

I make these doughnuts every time we have a snow day. It means I usually plan to be in the kitchen most of the day, but the reward is great. These doughnuts also freeze well to be enjoyed later—which is good, as it is a large recipe!

---

5 tablespoons active dry yeast

1 tablespoon sugar

1 cup warm water

1½ cup sugar

1 cup butter, softened

5 eggs, beaten

4 teaspoons salt

2 teaspoons vanilla extract

2 teaspoons ground nutmeg

15 cups unbleached white flour

4 cups water

oil or lard, for frying

Glaze

4 pounds powdered sugar

¼ cup cornstarch

2 cups milk

2 teaspoons vanilla extract

⅛ teaspoon salt

In a medium bowl, dissolve yeast and 1 tablespoon sugar in 1 cup warm water. Set aside.

In a very large bowl, cream 1½ cup sugar and butter with an electric hand mixer. Add eggs, salt, vanilla, and nutmeg. Mix until combined, then add yeast mixture. Add flour alternately with 4 cups water. I use my small hand mixer for the first few cups of flour, and then I use a wooden spoon to mix in the rest of the flour. This will be a fairly sticky dough, which makes a tender doughnut. Cover and let rise until doubled. Punch down, then let rise again until doubled.

Sprinkle flour on your workspace. Roll half the dough out to ½ inch thick. Cut circles with a doughnut cutter and lay on a lightly floured surface. Stretch out doughnut centers as you lay them down. This helps the hole to remain open as they rise. Repeat with remaining half of dough. Let rise until doubled in size.

In a large bowl, mix together glaze ingredients until smooth. Set aside.

In a deep electric skillet, heat lard or oil to 375°F.

Add doughnuts to skillet with the top, risen side facing down in the oil. This helps the bottom side to rise while you are frying the top side. Flip to fry each side until golden brown. Lay on paper towels for a minute or so.

Place doughnuts in rows on a wooden stick or wooden spoon handle. Lay across glaze bowl and pour glaze over doughnuts with a ladle. Let drip for a few minutes and then place on trays. Eat as many as you can; they are best when they are fresh! Freeze the rest in airtight containers for another snowy day.

TIP: It's important to maintain a temperature of 375°F when you are frying the doughnuts; at this temperature, the oil seals the outside of the doughnut so it doesn't soak in. If the oil is too hot, the doughnut will get too brown and crisp on the outside before the inside has cooked through. If the oil is not hot enough, the doughnut will absorb too much of the oil and the texture will be soggy and greasy.

Snow day

Every winter, on the first snow day, I make homemade doughnuts. It's something I started to do shortly after we were married, and I have been doing it ever since. Now, when it snows, Joshua hopes that maybe homemade doughnuts will appear.

We have six large bay windows across the front of our home, so it's so much fun to watch the snow fall. We usually have a fire crackling in our fireplace and plenty of hot drinks to sip. Being snowed in, sitting beside a cozy fire, sipping hot chocolate, eating fresh doughnuts: Joshua calls this his "Swiss Alps experience," and it's his idea of a perfect winter day.

But Caroline always manages to coax her dad to come outside to help make her a snowman. I get to enjoy watching them through the window. When they finally come in from the cold, they are more than ready to enjoy some fresh doughnuts and warm their toes by the fire.

PROTEIN BALLS

Makes about 25 balls

I've found myself mixing up this recipe many evenings after nine o'clock. It's usually because I'm hankering for a bedtime snack. These balls are also great for an afternoon pick-me-up with iced coffee. If you are rushed for time, you can skip melting the chocolate chips and just add them to the main filling.

1½ cup crispy rice cereal

1½ cup rolled oats

⅔ cup shredded sweetened coconut

½ cup dried cranberries

¼ teaspoon salt

1 cup peanut butter

½ cup honey

2 tablespoons protein powder (optional)

Topping

½ cup semisweet chocolate chips

sea salt

Using a stand mixer fitted with the paddle attachment, mix together all ingredients except those for topping until well combined. Using a small cookie scoop, form balls. Place on a baking sheet lined with parchment paper. Place in the freezer until firm, about 10 minutes.

Melt chocolate chips and drizzle over protein balls with a fork. Sprinkle with sea salt.

THREE-COLORED COCONUT CANDY

Makes 1 (9 x 13-inch) pan

Three-colored coconut candy is Joshua's favorite Christmas candy. It is a wonderful candy with an interesting texture—the gelatin makes it slightly spongy.

First layer

1½ tablespoon unflavored gelatin

3 tablespoons water

2 cups sugar

1 cup milk

1 tablespoon butter

dash salt

1¼ cup shredded sweetened
    coconut

1 teaspoon vanilla extract

Second layer

1½ tablespoon unflavored gelatin

3 tablespoons water

2 cups sugar

1 cup milk

1 tablespoon butter

dash salt

1¼ cup shredded sweetened
    coconut

1 teaspoon vanilla extract

⅛ teaspoon red food color

Third layer

1½ tablespoon unflavored gelatin

3 tablespoons water

2 cups sugar

1 cup milk

1 tablespoon butter

dash salt

1¼ cup shredded sweetened
    coconut

1 teaspoon vanilla extract

3 tablespoons cocoa powder

All three layers use the same base mixture, but the second and third layers include the addition of red food color and cocoa powder, respectively. Thus you will prepare a variation of the base layer three times.

In a small bowl, dissolve 1½ tablespoon gelatin in 3 tablespoons water and set aside.

In a medium saucepan, combine sugar, milk, butter, and salt and heat to boiling. Stirring constantly, boil to 232°F. Remove from heat.

Using a stand mixer fitted with the wire whip, add dissolved gelatin to mixing bowl and pour in hot sugar-and-milk mixture. Mix on medium-high for about 4 minutes. The mixture will turn white and creamy. Add coconut and vanilla. Beat until coconut is mixed in.

Pour into greased 9 x 13-inch dish. (The mixture will be similar to melted marshmallows—you will have to get a spoon and spread it out.)

Repeat instructions two more times, one for each layer. For the second layer, add red food color along with the coconut and vanilla. For the third layer, add cocoa powder along with the coconut and vanilla.

When set, invert 9 x 13-inch dish onto a cutting board. Cut into small pieces. Store in resealable plastic bags and freeze to retain freshness.

PEANUT BUTTER BALLS

Makes 3–4 dozen

Here is a simple candy I make every Christmas. Adding the cream cheese to the filling helps keep these candies nice and creamy.

3½ cups powdered sugar

1½ cup peanut butter

4 ounces cream cheese, softened

½ cup butter, softened

1 teaspoon vanilla extract

¼ teaspoon salt

Coating

dark chocolate, melted

milk chocolate, melted

fleur de sel or sea salt

Make balls: Mix together ingredients with hands until blended. Refrigerate for 10–15 minutes, or until firm. Use a small cookie scoop to form balls. Place on waxed paper and place in freezer until firm.

Dip into melted dark chocolate, then return to freezer until hardened. Drizzle with milk chocolate. Sprinkle with sea salt. Store in the freezer.

CHOCOLATE BARK

Serves 6

I make chocolate bark every Christmas. It's easy to make, and it's so good. I usually give a box of homemade candy to family members. I include this chocolate bark, peanut butter balls, and three-colored coconut candy.

10 ounces dark chocolate

10 ounces milk chocolate

½ cup coarsely chopped dried cranberries

½ cup chopped pecans

fleur de sel or sea salt

fresh orange zest

In a double boiler, melt dark chocolate. Pour melted chocolate into the middle of a baking sheet lined with parchment paper. Spread into a rectangle 3–4 inches from the edge of the tray. Place tray in the freezer to chill.

In a double boiler, melt milk chocolate. Remove tray from the freezer and pour three-quarters of the milk chocolate over the dark chocolate, spreading to the edges of the hardened chocolate. Sprinkle on dried cranberries and pecans. With a fork, drizzle the remaining milk chocolate across the rectangle, then sprinkle with fleur de sel. Finally, grate on some fresh orange zest. Place in the freezer until set, then break into pieces.

Box for a Christmas gift or place in the freezer for later.

CANNING AND MISCELLANY

Canning and preserving your own fruits and vegetables in the summer is deeply satisfying, but it can be exhausting as well. It always seems that you have the biggest picking of beans on the day you are the busiest with other tasks. But then you remember how much you enjoy green beans in the middle of the winter, and how much nourishment your family receives from them as well. There is truly nothing like sparkling jars of colorful produce as a result of your labor.

Canning times are subject to change according to USDA regulations. For the latest canning times, check your county extension office or the National Center for Food Preservation website.

Sour Cherry Pie Filling

Sweet Dill Pickles

Roasted Tomato Soup

Pizza Sauce

Canned Chunked Tomatoes

Taco Seasoning

Pork Rub

Sour cherry picking

There is nothing quite like a sour cherry pie. You have the tartness of the cherries paired with the sweetness of the thickening. A layer of flaky pie crust ties all those wonderful flavors together.

There is also nothing quite like harvesting sour cherries. In our area they are usually ready at the end of June, when it's hot. Mom and I will head up the road to a neighbor's small orchard that has two sour cherry trees. Picking sour cherries requires either climbing a tall ladder or being lifted up into the top of the tree in a skid-loader bucket. I prefer picking from the skid-loader bucket, because you can stand and have both hands free for picking. While I am in the top of the tree, I try not to think about how high I am off the ground—or how cherry juice is dripping from my elbows. I think about that cherry pie my family will enjoy in the middle of winter.

After our buckets are full, Mom and I head to her house to pit each cherry by hand. It's a good time to prop up your feet and catch up with family. We use a hairpin (a clean one, of course!) to remove each pit. We can some in a sweet thickening (recipe on p. 294) so that it's ready to use in a pie or on top of a dessert, and then we freeze some plain in freezer bags.

I look forward to picking sour cherries each year. When someone comments on my sour cherry pie filling, I usually tell them that I touched each of those cherries twice: once when I picked it, and once when I removed the pit.

In other words, these cherries are filled with lots of love. When you gather and preserve something like this, it holds memories that cherries from the grocery store just can't.

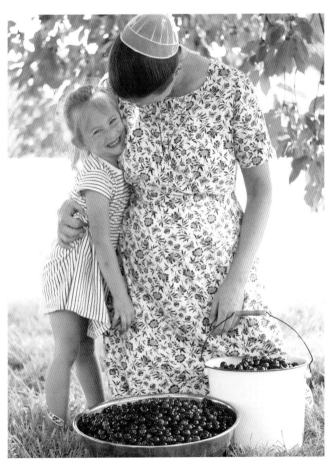

SOUR CHERRY PIE FILLING

Makes 8 quarts

This recipe makes a colorful and handy pie filling that you can use in the winter to make pies or other desserts. I like to use a few pints for cheesecake topping or anytime I'm in need of a colorful dessert garnish. You should be able to find Thermflo in most bulk food stores.

---

6 quarts sour cherries

6 cups water

6 cups sugar

1½ cup Thermflo (or Clear Jel)

1 teaspoon salt

1 teaspoon almond extract

1 tablespoon lemon juice

1½ teaspoon red food color

Pit the cherries; set aside. In a large pot, heat water, sugar, Thermflo, and salt until thickened. Remove from heat. Add almond extract, lemon juice, and food color. Fold in cherries.

Carefully fill sterilized canning jars. Tighten lids and process in a boiling water bath for 20 minutes.

SWEET DILL PICKLES

Makes 6 pints

These are my favorite pickles. They are great paired with sandwiches all year long. This is also the kind of pickle I use in Chicken Salad (p. 89).

---

12 fresh cucumbers (approximately)

6 grape leaves

6 fresh garlic cloves, peeled

6 fresh flowering dill sprigs

Syrup

2 cups sugar

2 tablespoons sea salt or pickling salt

1 cup white vinegar

3 cups water

Slice cucumbers ¼ inch thick (you can also slice into spears). Place 1 grape leaf, 1 garlic clove, and 1 dill sprig in the bottom of each sterilized pint jar.

In a saucepan, combine syrup ingredients and heat to boiling. Pour over cucumbers, leaving a 1-inch headspace. Place lids and tighten bands just until snug. Process in a boiling water bath for 10 minutes. For full flavor, allow to age for 2 weeks before opening.

TIP: The tannins in grape leaves help keep the pickles crisp. Also, a thicker-skinned cucumber stays crisper when pickled than those with thinner skins.

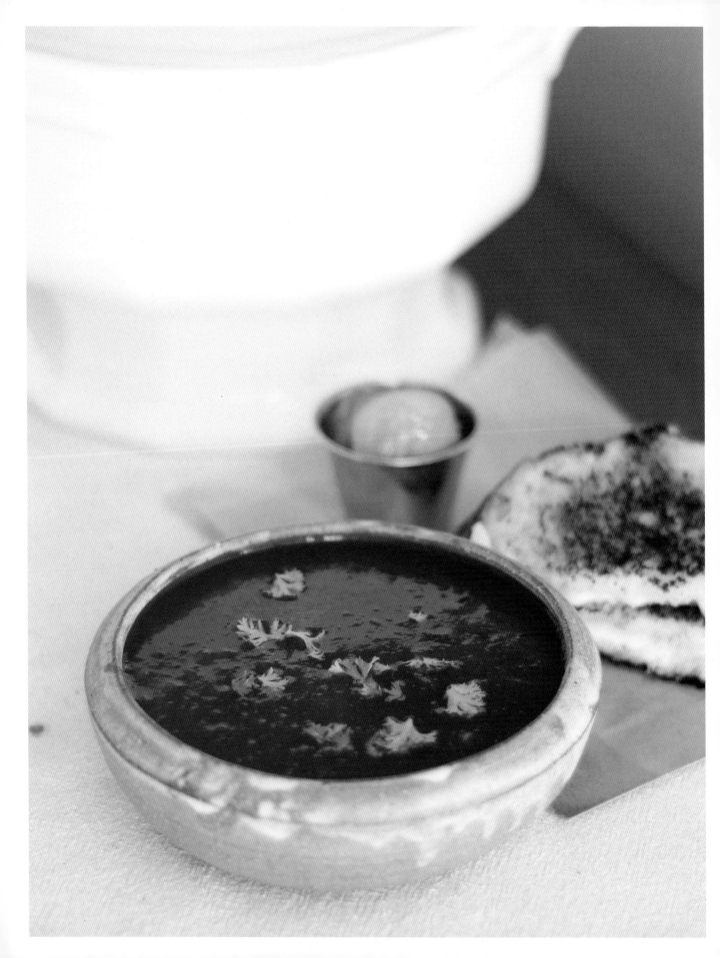

ROASTED TOMATO SOUP

Makes 6 quarts

This soup is great to have in your basement during the winter. Heat up a jar of it and serve with grilled cheese sandwiches. Drizzle a little cream into your soup bowl and be delighted.

4 gallons tomatoes, coarsely chopped

6 stalks celery, coarsely chopped

4 large bell peppers, coarsely chopped

4 onions, diced

¼ cup butter

⅔ cup sugar

¼ cup salt

1 tablespoon parsley flakes

⅛ teaspoon cayenne pepper

¼ cup Clear Jel

Divide tomatoes, celery, and bell peppers between two large roasting pans. Roast at 400°F for 1 hour. With an immersible blender, pulse the roasted tomatoes, celery, and peppers a few times to make it easier to run through the food mill. Run through a food mill.

Place diced onions on a baking sheet lined with parchment paper and roast at 400°F for 30 minutes.

In a large pot, combine tomato mixture and roasted onions. Add butter, sugar, salt, parsley flakes, and cayenne pepper and simmer for 20 minutes. Dissolve Clear Jel in a little water and add to soup to thicken.

Pour into sterilized quart jars. Process in a boiling water bath for 15 minutes.

PIZZA SAUCE

Makes 24 pints

This pizza sauce is packed with flavor and has a nice, thick consistency. It has the stamp of approval from Joshua, who is a pizza connoisseur.

---

4 bell peppers, chopped

8 onions, diced

2½ gallons thick tomato juice

1 cup oil, plus additional for sautéing

¾ cup sugar

½ cup salt

¼ cup dried basil

¼ cup dried oregano

2 tablespoons Italian seasoning

1 tablespoon red pepper flakes

2 teaspoons garlic powder

5 bay leaves, crumbled

3 cloves garlic, crushed

handful fresh basil, chopped

12 (6-ounce) cans tomato paste

In a large skillet, sauté bell peppers and onions with a little oil.

In a large stock pot, mix together tomato juice and remaining ingredients. Add sautéed peppers and onions. Simmer for 1 hour, stirring periodically to keep the bottom of the pot from scorching.

Pour into sterilized pint jars. Process in a boiling water bath for 15 minutes.

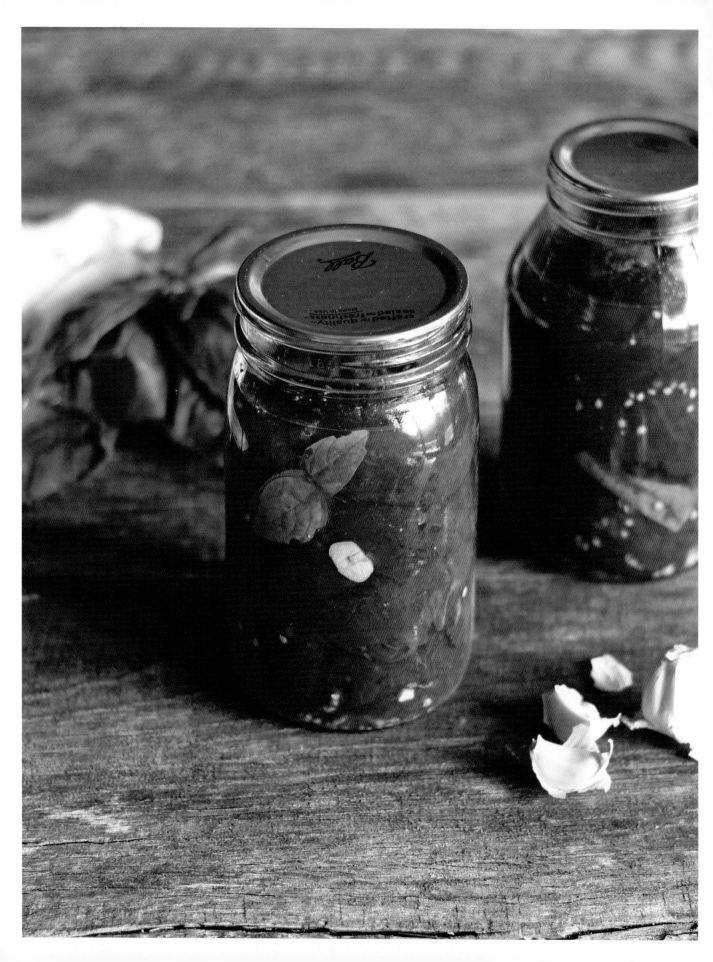

CANNED CHUNKED TOMATOES

This is more of a method than a recipe. Michelle, a friend from church, told me about this method, and it has came in handy for canning those few extra tomatoes you don't know what to do with. I then use these tomatoes in place of or along with tomato juice in recipes. I make a quick spaghetti sauce with the Italian version and add a can of tomato paste, ground beef, salt and pepper, and some cream.

tomatoes

salt

sugar

garlic cloves (optional)

fresh basil (optional)

In boiling water, scald tomatoes until their skins come off easily.

Core and chunk over a bowl to save the juice. Pack tomatoes into sterilized jars, leaving a 1-inch headspace. Add 1 teaspoon salt and 1 tablespoon sugar to each quart jar. Clean jar rim and put lids and rings in place. Process in a boiling water bath for 15 minutes.

For a savory Italian version: Add 1 crushed garlic clove to each jar and 4–5 leaves fresh basil. This version adds great flavor to tomato-based sauces.

TACO SEASONING

Once you make your own taco seasoning, you will always make your own! It's my secret ingredient in many taco dishes. One piece of advice: Be sure to buy quality spices. It will make all the difference.

¼ cup chili powder

2 tablespoons ground cumin

4 teaspoons salt

2 teaspoons black pepper

2 teaspoons paprika

1 teaspoon garlic powder

1 teaspoon dried oregano

½ teaspoon red pepper flakes (optional)

Place ingredients in a jar and shake well.

PORK RUB

Using this rub is like rubbing magic on pork. And when you start using it on pork, you will want to use it on every pork dish you make. It's that good. I use it on ribs, pork chops, pork roast, pork loin . . . am I missing any pork cuts?

3 tablespoons brown sugar

1 tablespoon salt

1 tablespoon pepper

Mix together ingredients, rub on pork, and prepare as usual for the dish you are making. If I remember in time, I put this rub on the pork several hours before cooking so that the flavors mingle. Be sure to refrigerate the pork if it will sit more than an hour before cooking.

KITCHEN TIPS AND MEASUREMENTS

TASTE YOUR FOOD AS YOU COOK

Even if I use the same recipe and follow it every time, I still always taste the final dish for salt and sprinkle in a little if needed. I think one of the things that makes a good cook is having the taste buds for the end result.

USE QUALITY SPICES

Spices are a small thing that make a big difference. Compare a generic brand and a name-brand spice; the color will be different, as will the smell and taste. Bulk food stores usually have quality spices at reasonable prices.

SHRED YOUR OWN CHEESE

It's cheaper per pound and tastes better. Once you get in the habit of shredding your own, you won't even be tempted to buy pre-shredded.

USE FRESH GARLIC

There is no comparison between the taste of fresh garlic and that of garlic powder. An easy way to peel a bunch of cloves at a time is to put them in a pint jar, cover with a lid, and shake vigorously. The skins will pop right off. A garlic press is a great way to crush garlic quickly and add it to a dish. Daintily mincing each clove with a knife is fine, but it takes time.

USE REAL BUTTERMILK

I know it's handy to quickly sour some milk with vinegar when a recipe calls for buttermilk. But it will never measure up to real buttermilk. Buttermilk will keep up to 3 weeks in the refrigerator.

TEST YOUR OVEN TEMPERATURE ACCURACY WITH A SEPARATE OVEN THERMOMETER

You can purchase them for under ten dollars. This eliminates lots of frustration for many cooks.

USE DIGITAL SCALES

These are especially helpful when feeding your sourdough starter equal amounts. One cup of water weighs more than one cup of flour. And if you shop at stores that sell groceries in bulk, after you're home it's handy to weigh out 8 ounces from a 32-ounce bag of something. I also use digital scales for weighing dough for pie crusts or shaping rolls to be sure they are equally divided.

Weights and measures

These are not exact equivalents, but have been rounded up or down for easier measuring.

⅛ teaspoon	0.5 ml	-	-
¼ teaspoon	1 ml	-	-
½ teaspoon	2 ml	-	-
1 teaspoon	5 ml	-	-
1 tablespoon	3 teaspoons	½ fluid ounce	15 ml
2 tablespoons	⅛ cup	1 fluid ounce	30 ml
4 tablespoons	¼ cup	2 fluid ounces	60 ml
5⅓ tablespoons	⅓ cup	3 fluid ounces	80 ml
8 tablespoons	½ cup	4 fluid ounces	120 ml
10⅔ tablespoons	⅔ cup	5 fluid ounces	160 ml
12 tablespoons	¾ cup	6 fluid ounces	180 ml
16 tablespoons	1 cup	8 fluid ounces	240 ml
2 cups	1 pint	-	-
2 pints	1 quart	-	-
4 quarts	1 gallon	-	-
28 grams	1 ounce	-	-
1 kilogram	2.2 pounds	-	-
1 liter	1 quart	-	-
4 liters	1 gallon	-	-

USE A DIGITAL INSTANT-READ THERMOMETER

I frequently use a thermometer for testing to see if things are done. For instance, bread is done at 195°F and meat loaf is done at 160°F. Even though Grandma always baked meat loaf for an hour at 350°F, a 1-pound loaf is actually done in around 35 minutes. You will find meat loaf and meatballs are more tender and less dense when not overbaked. A thermometer also eliminates the guessing game for when meats are done. Even though my mom still thinks pork chops can't be a bit pink, I remind her that when the thermometer reaches 145°F, they are safe for her to eat and serve.

Minimum internal temperatures
Source: fsis.usda.gov

Beef, Pork, Veal & Lamb Steaks, chops, roasts	145°F (62.8°C) and allow to rest for at least 3 minutes
Ground Meats	160°F (71.1°C)
Ham fresh or smoked (uncooked)	145°F (62.8°C) and allow to rest for at least 3 minutes
Fully Cooked Ham (to reheat)	Reheat cooked hams packaged in USDA-inspected plants to 140°F (60°C) and all others to 165°F (73.9°C).
All Poultry (breasts, whole bird, legs, thighs, wings, ground, giblets, and stuffing)	165°F (73.9°C)
Eggs	160°F (71.1°C)
Fish & Shellfish	145°F (62.8°C)
Leftovers	165°F (73.9°C)
Casseroles	165°F (73.9°C)

Oven temperature equivalents

250°F	120°C
275°F	135°C
300°F	150°C
325°F	160°C
350°F	180°C
375°F	190°C
400°F	200°C
425°F	220°C
450°F	230°C
475°F	240°C

CREATE A BAKING CORNER IN YOUR KITCHEN

I love to bake. My sister Faith claimed she didn't. Every time I went to bake something in her kitchen, I went zigzagging across her kitchen to find oats, oil, and flour. I told her that I wouldn't like baking either if I had to run everywhere to find my ingredients! So I went to her home one day and helped make her a baking corner, in which all her baking ingredients would be within arm's reach. I labeled quart jars and poured a common baking ingredient in each one. We moved her mixer, measuring cups, and spoons to her new baking corner. She called the next day to say she was amazed at how enjoyable baking really was!

TEN TIPS TOWARD A TIDY REFRIGERATOR

1 BUY LESS
If you have a full and messy fridge, you are buying too much food. This is where discount grocery stores can get you in trouble. You buy hickory, honey, and spicy barbecue sauce because they're only 99 cents each. But you just need one kind; find a brand you like and stick with one bottle. Think the same way about salad dressings and many other condiments. Keep it simple.

2 KEEP A GROCERY LIST
This not only keeps your fridge from having duplicates; it also keeps you sane while shopping. Who wants to guess what you need while grocery shopping? If you don't have a list, you end up buying more than you need.

3 ADD NEW STAPLES WITH CARE
Learn to know what you use on a weekly basis. This is very important. You can try new things—but just one at a time. See how fast the new item gets eaten and if it should become a weekly staple. I recently added hummus, and love it for afternoon snacks. But the week it doesn't get eaten, off the list it goes.

4 USE UP YOUR INVENTORY
Make a meal based on what you have in your fridge. Trying new recipes, with ingredients you don't normally have on hand, can be fun. But remember: it can often mean ingredients piling up in your fridge that you wouldn't usually use and that may be there for a long time.

5 DON'T FIX TOO MUCH FOOD
Learn how to cook enough food for one meal plus one container of leftovers. Leftovers can get you in trouble. They take up space and usually get thrown away after they get moldy. Sometimes rather than throwing away leftovers later, it's best to throw them out—or better yet, compost them—right away. I am not promoting waste. But if you know no one is going to eat that small dish of leftover cooked broccoli, go ahead and dispose of it. This saves you from washing a slimy, stinky dish.

6 BE A SMART SHOPPER

Think: what is on the agenda for the week? If you have a busy week and have plans that involve eating meals elsewhere, don't buy that whole gallon of milk; buy a half gallon.

7 CATEGORIZE YOUR DRAWERS AND SHELVES

Keep certain types of food in certain parts of the refrigerator. Doing so makes it easy to see, at a glance, what you might need to buy. I have a cheese and meat drawer and a vegetable drawer. Before I go grocery shopping, I peek in the drawers to see what we need.

8 WIPE IT DOWN OFTEN

We all know how to do this. It's just a matter of doing it! If a jar pulls up slowly because of pickle juice, get out your dishcloth and wipe it away. If you spill something, wipe it up right away. I often take my dishcloth and wipe off the shelves and fridge doors. This only takes a few seconds and is well worth your time. It's called fridge maintenance, and it doesn't have to take hours. Just do it here and there while you're doing other tasks in your kitchen.

9 ORGANIZE AND CLEAN ONCE A WEEK

Had a busy week? Does your fridge look a mess? Grab a soapy cloth and open your fridge door. Start by taking out items that need to be thrown away or composted. Then organize what you want to keep, wiping shelves and drawers as you go. Having a clean fridge is a bit like getting a facial; it just gives you that extra lift.

10 KEEP YOUR PANTRY THE SAME WAY

Keeping a clean pantry requires a lot of the same tasks that keeping a clean refrigerator does. Buy less. Keep a grocery list. Use up inventory. Organize once a week. Also, stock your pantry according to seasons. For example, in the winter I use more chicken stock and beans. In the summer I don't need those items as much, because we eat a lot from the garden.

ACKNOWLEDGMENTS

The first thanks goes to my sister Faith, who told me I could do this project with young children. She also came many days to help with housework and to keep my girls while I wrote. She was also a great encourager and helped me to not overthink this book: just to do my best and be done.

Also, a big thank you to my husband, Joshua, who encouraged me through this whole project and told me I could do this cookbook. You and the girls were so patient about waiting on your supper while I photographed it fifty times before you could eat it. You will always be my favorite person to cook for.

To my own mom, Sandra, who taught me so much about food. I give you 90 percent of the credit for this cookbook. And to my dad, Elvin, who taught me that hard work never hurt anyone and to keep going until a project is done.

To my other sister, Charity, who encouraged me with phone calls from Indiana. I promise I don't mind if you still don't use my fajita recipe.

To my good mom friend Kim, who tested recipes and listened to my many cookbook dilemmas. Thanks for being a listening ear and encouraging me along the way.

A big thank you to all my recipe testers: Suetta, Angie, Kim, Jessica, Charity, and Faith. You don't know how much I valued your feedback while testing recipes. You helped with one of the biggest jobs I had. Thank you from the bottom of my heart.

The final and big thank you goes to my editor, Valerie. Your grace, wisdom, and patience throughout this project gave me the encouragement and insight I needed to press on.

INDEX

THE AUTHOR

Hope Helmuth is a Mennonite cook, mother, and blogger who enjoys creating recipes, entertaining guests, gardening, graphic design, and photography. She and her husband and two daughters live in the beautiful Shenandoah Valley of Virginia, where they own a toy store, Timeless Toys, and several other businesses. Connect with her at HopesTable.com or on Instagram or Facebook.